With a Mighty Hand

With a Mighty Hand

The Story in the Torah

ADAPTED BY
Amy Ehrlich

PAINTINGS BY
Daniel Nevins

CANDLEWICK PRESS

First edition 2013

Library of Congress Catalog Card Number 2012947723
ISBN 978-0-7636-4395-9

13 14 15 16 17 18 TLF 10 9 8 7 6 5 4 3 2 1

Printed in Dongguan, Guangdong, China

This book was typeset in Centaur MT.
The illustrations were done in oil on wood.

Candlewick Press
99 Dover Street
Somerville, Massachusetts 02144

visit us at www.candlewick.com

For my grandsons: Aaron, Noah, and Gabriel

A. E.

For Ruby Brigmon, wherever you are

D. N.

CONTENTS

GENESIS

At the Beginning

Abraham

Jacob

Joseph

EXODUS

In Egypt

In the Wilderness

At Sinai

LEVITICUS

NUMBERS

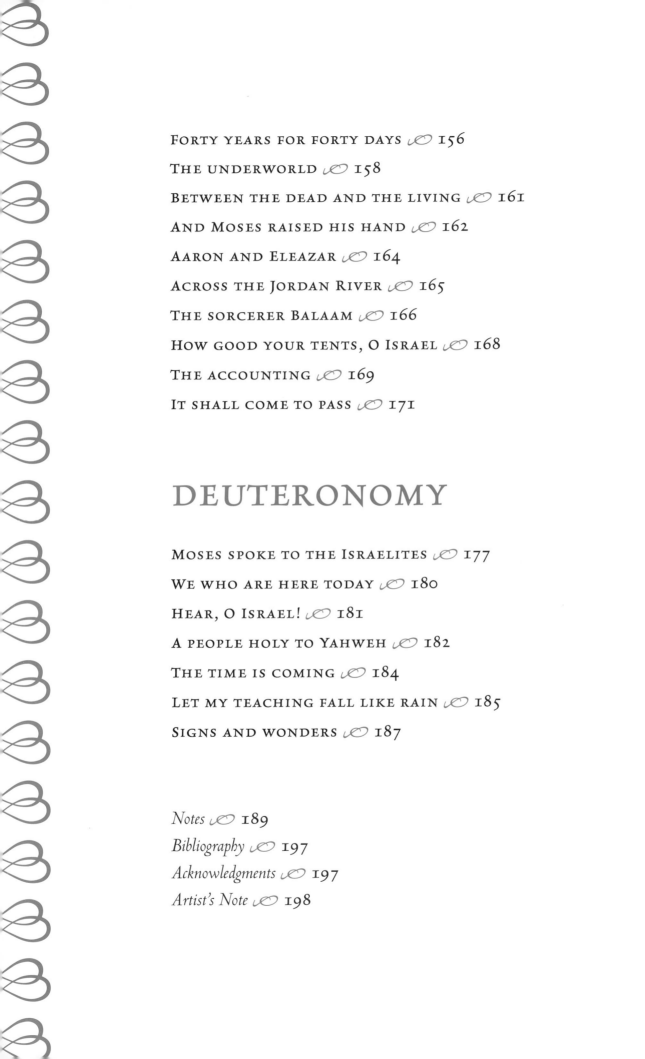

DEUTERONOMY

I remember the first Torah I ever saw. I was five years old, allowed to go to synagogue with my parents for the first time. The Torah was covered in a white satin cloth embroidered with silver thread and seed pearls. A silver shield protected it. The handles of the rolled-up Torah scroll had silver covers with tiny bells that tinkled as it was taken from the Ark in our synagogue. Men on the *bima* held the Torah high. The people in the congregation stood before it, chanting Hebrew prayers. I wanted to touch the Torah and play with it. I felt dizzy with longing.

In Judaism, a religion that forbids the worship of images or idols, the Torah is a sacred object, revered as the Word of God. Its name in Hebrew means "Teaching" or "Law." It is the story of the beginning of the Jewish people, their relationship to God, and what they must do to please God. Five books make up the Torah: Genesis, Exodus, Leviticus, Numbers, and Deuteronomy. They are the first part of the Hebrew Bible, which Christians call the Old Testament.

In the Torah are God's commandments — not just the ten famous ones, but 613 laws and prohibitions about every aspect of life. Many of these, such as how goats and rams should be slaughtered and what parts of animals are clean and unclean, might seem strange and primitive. But others express profound assumptions about human beings and how we should treat one another. The Torah says that we are created in God's image and therefore share God's nature. It says human life is sacred. The ethical system the Torah has given us has endured in the West for thousands of years. We are still attempting to live by its laws.

Another world-changing inheritance from the Hebrew Bible is monotheism, the belief in one god that Christianity and Islam share with Judaism. Many people believe monotheism began in Genesis with the creation. But that is not true. There are references in Genesis and throughout the Torah to other gods who were thought to exist side by side with God. They were not to be worshipped; only God was to be worshipped. This belief is called henotheism. In later books of the Hebrew Bible, other gods drop away, and God is God alone. The first line of liturgy Jewish children learn is the *Shema*, which means "to hear" in Hebrew: "Hear, O Israel! The Lord, our God, the Lord is One."

What was the world like before the Torah? I try to imagine it. A vast starry sky, a desolate land, a small tribe of nomads wandering with their tents and herds. For these people, our ancestors, life must have seemed frightening and arbitrary. Idols and household gods might be of comfort, but there was little an individual could do to alter fate. And then along came Abraham the patriarch, to whom God said, "Go forth from your land . . . to a land I will show you. I will make you a great nation, and I will bless you." So the Torah tells us, and again I imagine it. Such a voice! Coming out of such an emptiness!

It was the beginning of the covenant between God and God's people, an agreement similar to a legal treaty. If Abraham did what God wanted, God would favor him. Soon God demanded that Abraham

and his sons and the slaves in his household be circumcised, the blood and the flesh a sign of the covenant.

Abraham did it. He followed God, and so did Abraham's son Isaac, his grandson Jacob, and his great-grandson Joseph. But the land they were promised eluded them. Joseph was sold into slavery in Egypt, and many generations later, Abraham's descendants were all enslaved by the pharaoh. Then came Moses, who led them out of Egypt to Mount Sinai, where they received God's commandments, then into the wilderness, where they disobeyed God and wandered in punishment for forty years. By this time they were a nation, hundreds of thousands of people: the Israelites. They had not reached the promised land, but God was still in their midst.

When I set out to write a version of the Torah, I soon determined that my best way forward would be to follow the thread of its story. I would tease this out little by little and go wherever the story led me. Inevitably, this being the Torah, it led me through thickets of genealogy, law, and ritual. I've included portions of these—enough, I hope, to give readers a sense of how the ancient Israelites experienced their faith, and how some observant Jews still do.

Anyone who reads the Torah will see that a lot of it doesn't make sense. It is repetitive, inconsistent, even contradictory. The Torah's fractured history may be responsible. Although the events in it could have occurred from about 2000 BCE to 1250 BCE (meaning "Before the Common Era," a term preferred by Jewish historians to *BC*, "Before Christ"), they were not written down until about 900 BCE to 450 BCE, when literacy in the eastern Mediterranean had become more widespread. (Two other great works of antiquity, Homer's epics the *Odyssey* and the *Iliad*, were compiled in Greece at the same time.)

The five books of the Torah began orally as tribal tales and were then written down out of sequence, and over and over again, by a series of authors or redactors with their own beliefs and motives. Many biblical scholars believe there are four principal sources of the Torah, each known by a letter abbreviation and presenting a different view of God and God's laws. "J" calls God Yahweh, "E" calls God Elohim, "D" is the source of the book of Deuteronomy, and "P" is the priestly and probably the most recent source.

The Torah was not completed until after the Babylonian conquest, in 586 BCE, when the Israelites became exiles and lost their first temple in Jerusalem. It was the beginning of the Jewish Diaspora, a scattering that continues to this day. Without leaders or the protection of a state, without a place to worship God, the Israelites relied on their laws and the record of their history in the Torah. They studied the Torah diligently; they wrote commentary upon commentary about it; they comforted themselves with its intricacies. Dwelling in the Torah, among God's commandments, the exiled Israelite remnant became truly "people of the book," a name Jews still carry on their wanderings. Their knowledge and steadfast belief have been a refuge, helping them survive centuries of anti-Semitism and persecution—ghetto, Inquisition, pogrom, and Holocaust.

Though there are some explanatory notes at the back of *With a Mighty Hand,* I've chosen to tell the Torah's story without interpretation, just as it is on the page. Beyond the illogic created by a series of authors writing over a long period of time, readers will discover many unsettling mysteries in the Torah. Why did God ask Abraham to sacrifice his son? Who wrestled with Jacob in the night? Why did God try to murder Moses after sending him back to Egypt? Why was Moses forbidden to enter the promised land? Scholars and theologians have argued these questions for centuries, but no one knows the answers. The Torah is not transparent. It continues to confound and shock us, and in this way it is ever new.

On many holidays and on Saturday mornings in my synagogue and in synagogues around the world, the Torah is taken from the Ark, uncovered, and unrolled. It is read on *Shabbat* from the beginning of Genesis to the end of Deuteronomy, a Torah portion every week throughout the year. Before and after the reading, the Torah scrolls are carried through the sanctuary to bring them closer to the congregation. Men touch the Torah with their prayer shawls, then kiss the fringes. Women touch their prayer books to it, then kiss the covers. I reach out with my prayer book. Tears sting my eyes. The longing I felt as a child in the presence of the Torah is with me still.

When I was working on *With a Mighty Hand,* I kept coming back to some words in Moses's first sermon to the Israelites in Deuteronomy. The generation that he led out of Egypt and that received the commandments at Sinai has died in the wilderness, but Moses says, "Learn the laws I speak and do them always. Yahweh, our God, made a covenant with us at Sinai. Not with our fathers did he make it but with us, the living — we who are here today."

What could that mean? I realized it wasn't only the children of the wilderness generation who were being addressed, but all of us. We are the children of our ancestors, carrying the weight and meaning of history. The Torah wants us to witness these events, to follow God's laws, to honor and keep the covenant.

We who are here today.

Amy Ehrlich
Barnet, Vermont

Who is like You among the gods, O Yahweh!

Who is like You, mighty in holiness,

awesome in splendor, worker of wonders!

——Exodus

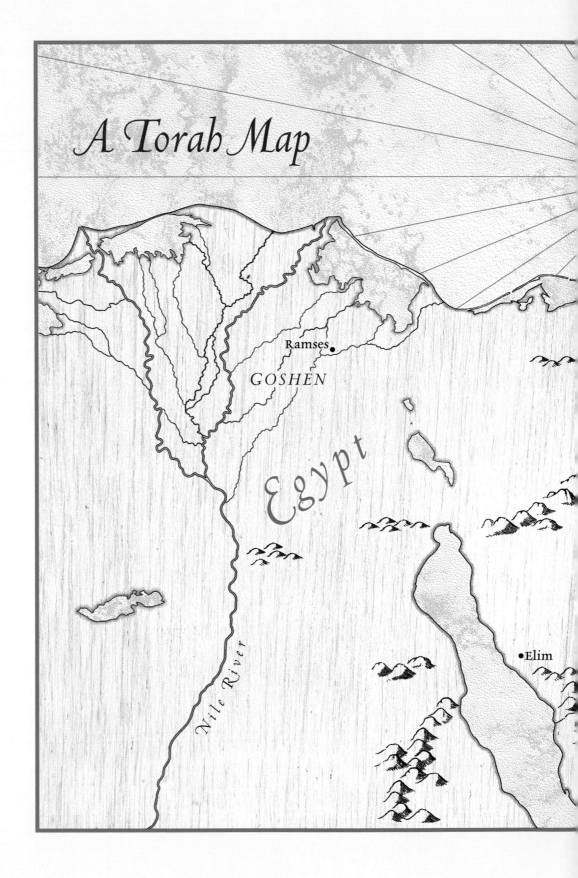

A Torah Map

Ramses

GOSHEN

Egypt

Nile River

•Elim

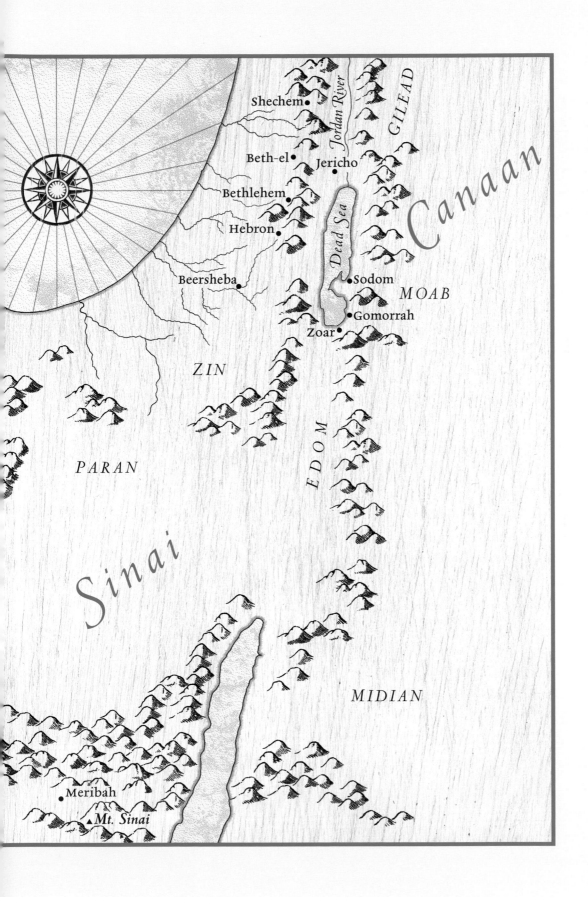

Shechem

Jordan River

GILEAD

Beth-el

Jericho

Canaan

Bethlehem

Dead Sea

Hebron

Sodom

MOAB

Beersheba

Gomorrah

Zoar

ZIN

EDOM

PARAN

Sinai

MIDIAN

Meribah

▲ Mt. Sinai

A Torah Genealogy

THE PATRIARCHS

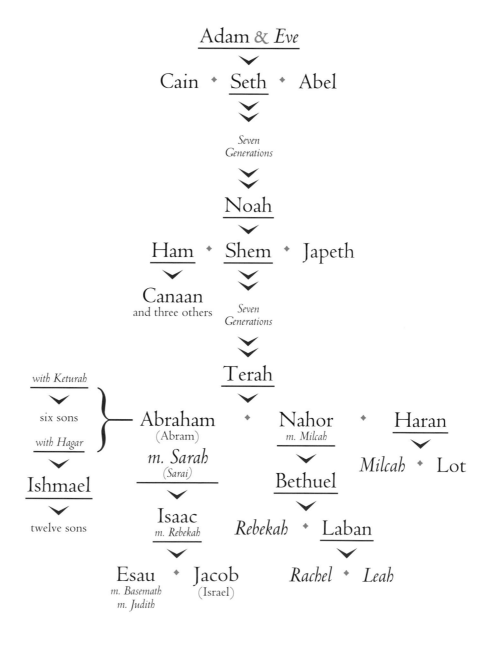

Adam & *Eve*

Cain ◆ Seth ◆ Abel

Seven Generations

Noah

Ham ◆ Shem ◆ Japeth

Canaan
and three others

Seven Generations

Terah

with Keturah
six sons
with Hagar

Abraham
(Abram)
m. Sarah
(Sarai)

◆ Nahor
m. Milcah
◆ Haran

Milcah ◆ Lot

Bethuel

Ishmael

Isaac
m. Rebekah

Rebekah ◆ Laban

twelve sons

Esau
m. Basemath
m. Judith
◆ Jacob
(Israel)

Rachel ◆ *Leah*

THE TWELVE TRIBES OF ISRAEL

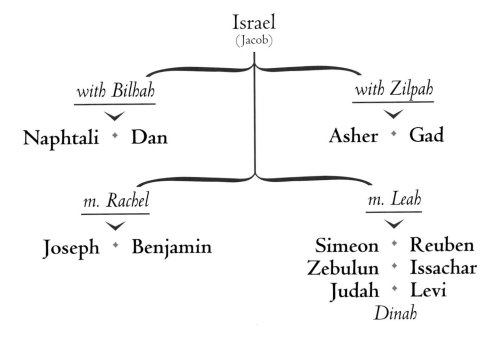

Israel
(Jacob)

with Bilhah

Naphtali ◆ Dan

with Zilpah

Asher ◆ Gad

m. Rachel

Joseph ◆ Benjamin

m. Leah

Simeon ◆ Reuben
Zebulun ◆ Issachar
Judah ◆ Levi
Dinah

DESCENDANTS OF LEVI

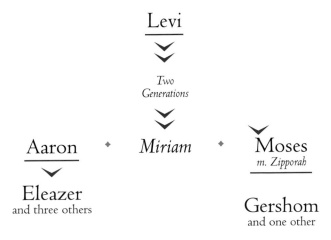

Levi

*Two
Generations*

Aaron ◆ *Miriam* ◆ Moses
m. Zipporah

Eleazer
and three others

Gershom
and one other

GENESIS

בראשית

At the Beginning

LET THERE BE LIGHT!

At the beginning, the earth was wild and empty, with darkness
sweeping over the water.
God said, "Let there be light!" And there was light.
Then God separated the light from the darkness.
God called the light Day. And the darkness He called Night.
Evening came and morning—the first day.

God said, "Let there be a dome to separate water from water."
And He called the dome Sky.
Evening came and morning—the second day.

God said, "Let the water be gathered up and dry land appear."
And it was so.
The dry land He called Earth. The water He called Seas.
God said, "Let the earth sprout plants — seed plants and fruit trees."
And He saw that it was good.
Evening came and morning — the third day.

God said, "Let there be lights in the sky to shine upon the earth."
He made a great light for day and a smaller one for night,
and he made the stars.
Evening came and morning — the fourth day.

God said, "Let the seas swarm with living creatures
and let birds fly above the earth."
Then He created the sea serpents and the winged birds.
And it was so.
Evening came and morning — the fifth day.

God said, "Let the earth bring forth cattle
and creeping things and wild beasts."
And it was so.
Then God said, "Let humans have dominion
over all the living creatures."
And He created humans in His image.
In the image of God He created them: man and woman.
And He blessed them and said, "Be many and fill the earth.
I give you every green plant and tree fruit.
They shall be yours for food."
And it was so.
Now God saw all that He had made, and it was very good.
Evening came and morning — the sixth day.

FROM THE DUST OF THE EARTH

Thus were made heaven and earth, with all their splendor.
On the seventh day, God ended the work He had been doing.
And He blessed that day and called it holy.

At the time of Yahweh's making of earth and heaven,
He made the man from the dust of the earth: *adamah.*
Yahweh blew into his nostrils the breath of life,
and the man became a living being.
Yahweh planted a garden in Eden, to the east,
and there He placed the man He had made.
Then He commanded the man,
"From every tree in the garden you may eat.
But from the tree of knowledge you must not.
For if you eat from it, you will surely die."

Now Yahweh said, "It is not good for the man to be alone.
I will make him a companion."
From the earth Yahweh formed all the birds and beasts
and He brought them to the man one by one.
And whatever the man called each creature, that became its name.
But no companion for the man was found,
so Yahweh made a deep sleep fall upon him.
Yahweh took one of the man's ribs and closed up the flesh.
Then He formed the rib into a woman and brought her to the man.
The man said:
> "This one at last
> is bone of my bones
> and flesh of my flesh.
> This one shall be called Woman,
> for from Man she was taken."

The two of them, the man and the woman, were naked,
yet they felt no shame.

THE TREE OF KNOWLEDGE

Now, the serpent was the slyest of all the wild beasts
that Yahweh had made.
It said to the woman, "I know God said you must not eat
from the tree of knowledge, or you will die.
But you will not die.
Instead, your eyes will be opened and you will become like gods,
knowing good and evil."
Then the woman took the fruit and ate it and gave it also to the man,
and he ate.
And their eyes were opened and they saw that they were naked
and they covered themselves with fig leaves.

The breeze came up, and they heard Yahweh walking in the garden.
The man and woman hid themselves among the trees.
Yahweh called to them, "Where are you hiding?"
The man said, "I was afraid because I was naked."
Yahweh said, "Who told you that?
Have you eaten from the tree that was forbidden?"
The man said, "The woman You gave me — she gave me the fruit."
And the woman said, "The serpent tempted me, and so I ate."

Then Yahweh said to the serpent:
> "Because you have done this, you will crawl
> upon your belly.
> Dust will you eat, all the days of your life."

Then to the woman He said:

> "I will multiply the pain of your childbirth.
>
> In pain will you bear children."

To Adam He said:

> "The ground will be cursed.
>
> By hard labor will you till it.
>
> By the sweat of your brow will you eat bread
>
> until you return to the ground,
>
> for dust you are
>
> and to dust will you return."

Then Yahweh clothed Adam and the woman in garments of skin
and sent them away from the garden, east of Eden.

CAIN AND THEN ABEL, TWO SONS

The man called the woman *Eve:* life giver,
for she became mother of all the living.
She gave birth to Cain and then Abel, two sons.
Years passed and Cain brought Yahweh a gift, fruit from the soil.
And Abel brought Him a firstborn from his flock.
Yahweh was pleased with Abel and his gift.
But He was not pleased with Cain's gift.

Cain became angry and he looked away.
And Yahweh said:

> "Why are you angry?
>
> Why do you look away?
>
> If you do right, all will be well.
>
> But if you do not,
>
> sin waits for you, a crouching demon."

But Cain did not listen.

When they were out in the field, he rose up against Abel, his brother, and killed him.

Yahweh said to Cain, "Where is Abel, your brother?"

Cain said, "I do not know. Am I my brother's keeper?"

And Yahweh said, "What have you done?

Your brother's blood cries out to Me from the soil!

And now the soil that opened its mouth for your brother's blood will give you nothing.

No more will you till. You will be a wanderer on the earth."

Cain said, "My punishment is too great. Whoever comes upon me will kill me!"

"No," said Yahweh, and He put a mark on Cain, to protect him.

Adam's next son was Seth.

To Seth was born Enosh.

To Enosh was born Kenan.

To Kenan was born Mahalel.

To Mahalel was born Jared.

To Jared was born Enoch.

To Enoch was born Methuselah.

To Methuselah was born Lamech.

When Lamech had lived a hundred and eighty-two years,
a son was born to him.

Lamech called his name *Noah,* saying, "May this one comfort us
and heal our hands from work in the ground
that Yahweh has cursed."

When Noah had lived five hundred years, he had three sons:
Shem, Ham, and Japheth.

AN ARK OF GOPHER WOOD AND REEDS

Noah was a righteous man
and found favor with Yahweh in his generation.
But the earth was filled with evil. The earth had gone to ruin.
God spoke to Noah, saying,
"I will put an end to men, who have filled the earth with evil.
I will bring about the Flood, to destroy all flesh under the sky.
But I will make my covenant with you.
Make yourself an ark of gopher wood and reeds.
Make an opening for daylight in it and an entrance.
Come into the ark, with your sons, your wife, and your sons' wives.
Take two of every living creature, male and female,
to remain alive with you—
two of every bird, every herd animal, every creeping thing.
Gather food for you and for them."
Noah did it, all that God commanded.

FORTY DAYS AND FORTY NIGHTS

After seven days, the Flood was upon the earth.
In the six hundredth year of Noah's life,
in the second month, on the seventeenth day,
            all the waters of the ocean burst apart
            and the floods of heaven broke open.
The rain fell for forty days and forty nights.
The water lifted the ark, so that it floated above the earth.
The high mountains were covered
and all the living creatures that swarmed upon the earth were killed—
birds and cattle, beasts and humans.
Noah alone was saved, and those who were with him in the ark.

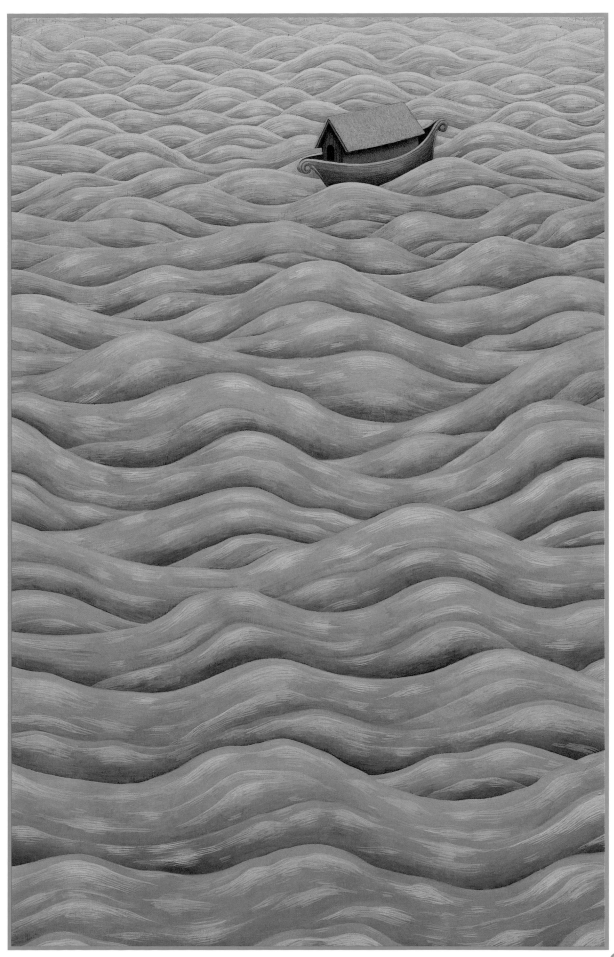

Then God brought a rushing wind across the earth

and the ark came to rest on the mountains of Ararat.

Noah sent out a dove to see if there was a resting place for her.

But the waters were still upon the earth.

After seven days, Noah sent her out again.

The dove returned at evening.

And here! An olive leaf was in her beak.

Noah knew that the waters had dropped down.

He sent the dove out, and she did not return.

Then Noah, with his sons and his wife and his sons' wives,

and with all living creatures — birds, herd animals, creeping things —

came from the ark.

Noah built an altar and he sacrificed pure animals and pure birds,

burning them as an offering to God.

Yahweh smelled the sweet smoke and said,

"Never again will I curse the ground

because what the human heart plans is evil from its youth.

Never again will I doom living beings.

Never again.

>On all the days of the earth,
>
>planting and harvest,
>
>cold and heat,
>
>summer and winter
>
>shall not cease."

AFTER THE FLOOD

Now God blessed Noah and his sons and said to them,

"Be many and swarm upon the earth!

All creatures on the soil and fish in the sea,

with the green plants, they shall be yours to eat.

But whoever sheds human blood,

for that, his blood will be shed,

for in God's image, God made humankind."

And again God spoke to Noah and his sons, saying,

"I will make my covenant with you and all your children to come.

Never again will there be a flood to destroy the earth.

My bow will be in the clouds

as a sign of the covenant between God and the generations—

all flesh that is upon the earth."

Noah's sons who came out of the ark were Shem, Ham, and Japheth.

And Ham was the father of Canaan.

Noah planted a vineyard and he became drunk from the wine.

He was naked in his tent when Ham entered there and saw him.

Ham told his brothers, but they held a cloth and walked backward

so that they did not see their father's nakedness.

Now, when Noah awoke and learned what Ham had done,

he cursed Ham's son Canaan, saying:

"Cursed be Canaan;

a slave shall he be to his brothers."

Noah's days were nine hundred and fifty years, and then he died.

After the Flood, the generations of the sons of Noah

spread across the earth.

At that time, all the people had one language and the same words.

As they traveled from the east, they found a valley

in Shinar and settled there.

They said to one another, "Come! Let us bake bricks

and burn them black.

Then let us build a city, and a high tower to show our glory,

and so that we will not be scattered across the earth."
But Yahweh came down to look at the city
and the tower that man had built.
He said, "If they are one people with one language,
then nothing will be out of their reach. They will stop at nothing.
Come! We will fracture their language
so that no man will understand another."
Thus Yahweh scattered them, and they had to stop building the city.
And its name was called Babel: *Babylon.*

This is the line of Shem:
Arpachshad, Shelah, Eber, Peleg, Reu, Serug, Nahor, Terah.
To Terah was born Abram, Nahor, and Haran —
ten generations from Noah.
Abram and Haran took wives, and Abram's wife was Sarai.
Sarai was barren. She had no child.

And Terah took his son Abram and Sarai, his daughter-in-law,
along with his grandson Lot,
and they set out from Ur of the Chaldeans to the land of Canaan.
But when they reached Haran, they settled there.
The days of Terah were two hundred and five years,
and he died in Haran.

Abraham

GO FORTH

And now Yahweh said to Abram,
"Go forth from your land, from your kinsmen,
from your father's house, to a land I will show you.

> I will make you a great nation,
> And I will bless you.
> I will make your name great,
> and you will be a blessing.
> I will bless those who bless you.
> And those who curse you, I will curse.
> All the clans of the earth will be blessed through you."

Abram went forth, as Yahweh had commanded,
and he took Sarai, his wife, and Lot, his brother's son.
In Canaan, Abram spread his tent and built an altar to Yahweh.
And he called out Yahweh's name.

There was a famine in the land,
and so Abram went down to Egypt to sojourn there,
for the famine was harsh.
When he came near Egypt, he said to Sarai, his wife,
"I know you are beautiful to look at,
and when the Egyptians see that you are my wife,
they will kill me and take you for their own.
Say, then, that you are my sister so that they will let me live."

And it happened that when Abram came into Egypt,
Pharaoh's servants saw that Sarai was beautiful
and they took her to Pharaoh for a wife.
And on Sarai's account, Abram was given sheep and oxen,
donkeys and camels, and many slaves.

But Yahweh struck Pharaoh and his household with plagues
because of Sarai.
Then Pharaoh had Abram brought to him.
"What is this you have done to me?" he asked.
"Why did you say, 'She is my sister,' so I took her for a wife?
Now here is your wife. Take her and go!"
Pharaoh sent guards to put Abram out
with Sarai and all that he had.

AND HE CALLED OUT YAHWEH'S NAME

Abram traveled up from Egypt, he and his wife, to the Negev.

And Abram was laden with cattle and livestock, with silver and gold.

He went from the Negev to Canaan,

to the place where he had built an altar to Yahweh.

And he called out Yahweh's name.

Lot, who came with Abram, also had cattle and livestock and tents.

The land could not support them both, to dwell together.

Abram said to Lot, "Let there be no quarreling between us,

for we are kinsmen.

Isn't the whole plain before you? Let us separate."

Lot lifted his eyes and saw the plain of the Jordan—

how well watered it was, like Yahweh's garden in Eden,

like Egypt itself.

So Lot chose the plain of the Jordan and they parted.

Abram dwelled in the land of Canaan.

And Lot dwelled in the cities of the plain,

spreading his tent near Sodom,

though the men of Sodom were wicked and sinful before Yahweh.

When Lot had gone, Yahweh said to Abram,

"Lift up your eyes and see where you are.

North and south, east and west, all the land you see,

I give to you and your children forever.

And your children will be measureless, like the dust of the earth.

Up! Walk through the land in its width and distance,

for to you I will give it."

And Abram came to dwell near the terebinths of Mamre,

which are in Hebron, and he built an altar to Yahweh.

COUNT THE STARS

Some time later, the word of Yahweh came to Abram in a vision:

> "Fear not, Abram,
>
> for I am a shield to you.
>
> Your reward shall be great."

Abram said, "Yahweh, my God, what can you give me?

Am I not childless? When I die, my servant Eliezer will be my heir."

And Yahweh said,

"That one shall not be your heir. Your own child will be heir to you."

He took Abram outside and said to him,

"Look at the sky and count the stars. Can you count them?

So shall your children be."

And Abram trusted in Yahweh.

Then Yahweh said to him,

"I am Yahweh who brought you out from Ur of the Chaldeans

to give you this land to inherit."

Abram said, "Yahweh, my God, when will it be mine?"

Yahweh said,

"Bring Me a young heifer, a she-goat and a ram,

a turtledove and a pigeon."

And he brought them.

Abram halved them down the middle and put each part

opposite to the other.

But the birds he did not halve.

Vultures flew at the carcasses, but Abram drove them away.

As the sun was setting, a deep sleep came over Abram.

And now fear and darkness were falling upon him.

And Yahweh said to him,

"You must know now,

know that your children will be strangers in a land not theirs.

They will be put into slavery and afflicted for four hundred years.

But upon the nation that afflicts them, I will bring judgment.

As for you—

you shall go to your fathers in peace.

You shall be buried in the ripeness of age.

And in the fourth generation, your children will return here."

Now, when it was dark night,

a smoking brazier and a fiery torch passed between

the halves of the animals.

Then Yahweh made a covenant with Abram, saying,

"I have given this land to your children,

from the river of Egypt to the great river, the river Euphrates."

A WILD ASS OF A MAN

Sarai, Abram's wife, had borne him no children.

She had an Egyptian slave girl. Her name was Hagar.

Sarai said to Abram, "Yahweh has kept me from bearing a child.

Come. Lie with my slave girl so that I may have a son through her."

Abram listened to Sarai's voice.

And Sarai took Hagar, her slave girl, and gave her to Abram as a wife.

Abram lay with Hagar and she conceived a child.

Then Sarai said to Abram, "Now that she is pregnant,

I am worthless in her eyes."

Abram said, "Look, your slave girl is in your hands.

Do what you like."

Then Sarai tormented Hagar so that the girl had to flee from her.

Yahweh's messenger found Hagar by a spring of water
in the wilderness.
He said, "Hagar, where have you come from,
and where are you going?"
She said, "I am fleeing from Sarai, my mistress."
Yahweh's messenger said to Hagar,
"Return to her and let yourself be tormented by her hand."
And he said:

> "I will make your children many,
> too many to count."

And he said:

> "Here. You are pregnant,
> you will bear a son.
> Call his name *Ishmael:* God hears.
> He shall be a wild ass of a man,
> his hand against everyone,
> everyone's hand against him.
> Yet he will dwell with his brothers."

Hagar bore Abram a son, and
Abram called him Ishmael.
Abram was eighty-six years old
when Ishmael was born.

You shall be called Abraham

Now, when Abram was ninety-nine years old,
Yahweh appeared to him and said,
"I am your God.
Walk in My ways and be without blame."
Abram fell to his face on the ground.
Then God spoke again, saying:

> "No longer shall your name be called Abram.
> You shall be called *Abraham:* father of many nations.
> I will make you fruitful.
> And make a throng of nations of you.
> And kings shall come forth from you.

This is my covenant that you are to keep, between Me and you,
and your sons after you, throughout the generations:
Every male among you shall be circumcised at eight days old
so that in your flesh will be a sign of the covenant between us.
And your slaves shall be circumcised, too,
and those bought from foreigners."

God also said to Abraham,
"As for your wife, she shall no longer be called Sarai,
but her name shall be *Sarah:* princess.
I will bless her,
and I will give you a son from her.
Nations and kings shall come from her."

But Abraham laughed, saying to himself:

> "To a man of one hundred years shall a child be born?
> Or to Sarah, a woman of ninety?"

And he said to God,
"I would be glad if Ishmael only might live by your favor."

God said,

"Still, Sarah, your wife, is to give birth to a son.

You shall call his name *Isaac:* he laughs.

I will make my covenant with him for the ages.

But I will bless Ishmael, too."

On that same day, Abraham was circumcised,

and he took Ishmael, his son, and the slaves in his household

and circumcised them as God had said.

Abraham was ninety-nine years old when he was circumcised,

and Ishmael, his son, was thirteen.

In the heat of the day

Yahweh appeared to Abraham near the terebinths of Mamre,

where Abraham was sitting by his tent in the heat of the day.

Abraham raised his eyes, and three men stood there.

He ran toward them and bowed to the ground, saying,

"My lords, if I have found favor with you,

please do not pass by your servant.

Bathe your feet and rest under a tree.

I will bring you water, and bread to eat."

Then Abraham ran into the tent to Sarah and said,

"Hurry! Knead three measures of flour and make bread loaves!"

And Abraham ran to the herd and chose a tender young ox

for a serving boy to prepare.

And he brought curds and milk and the meat of the ox

and set these before the men.

He stood near them under the tree as they ate.

They said to him, "Where is your wife, Sarah?"

Abraham said, "There, in the tent."

Then one man said, "I will return next year, and she will have a son."

Sarah was listening at the entrance to the tent,

and she laughed, saying, "How can I bear a child, old as I am?"

But Yahweh said to Abraham,

"Why does she laugh? Is anything beyond God?"

Sarah lied, saying, "No, I did not laugh," for she was afraid.

But He said,

"Yes, you laughed."

The men arose and set out toward Sodom

with Abraham walking alongside to show the way.

And Yahweh thought, "Shall I hide from Abraham what I will do?

For he is to become a great nation, and I have chosen him

so that he might keep the ways of God and do what is right and just."

So Yahweh said to Abraham, "The outcry in Sodom and Gomorrah
is too great,
and their sin weighs heavily upon me.
If the outcry is true — destruction!"
The men turned then and went to Sodom,
and Yahweh stood before Abraham.

Abraham drew close to Him and said,
"Will You destroy the innocent along with the guilty?
Perhaps there are fifty innocent men in the city.
Shouldn't the judge of all the earth act justly?"
Yahweh said,
"If I find fifty innocent men, I will forgive the whole city
for their sake."
Then Abraham said, "Here I speak to my God,
I who am but dust and ashes.
But if there were forty men who were innocent?
Or twenty? Or if there were only ten?"
And Yahweh said,
"I will not destroy the city for the sake of the ten."

THE MEN OF SODOM

The two messengers came into Sodom at sunset,
when Lot was sitting at the gate.
He rose to meet them and bowed low, saying,
"Now, my lords, you must turn aside to your servant's house
and bathe your feet and stay until morning."
He made them food and baked them bread and they ate.
But the men of the city, the men of Sodom, circled the house.
They called out to Lot, "We want the men who came tonight.

Give them to us."

Lot went out to them, shutting the door.

He said, "I pray you, my friends, do not be so wicked.

Do nothing to these men, for they have come

under the shadow of my roof beam.

I will bring you my two daughters who have never known a man.

You can have them instead."

But the men of Sodom pressed hard against Lot,

and moved to break down the door.

Then the messengers stretched out their hands

and pulled Lot inside the house.

And the men who were at the entrance were struck with dazzling light.

All of them, young and old, were blinded and helpless.

Then the messengers said to Lot, "Who else do you have?

Your sons and daughters, take them away,

for Yahweh has sent us to destroy the city."

Lot went out and spoke to his sons-in-law,

who had married his daughters.

But they did not believe him, and Lot himself delayed.

As dawn broke, the messengers seized Lot's hand and his wife's hand

and the hands of their two daughters remaining.

And in God's mercy, they led Lot's family out of the city.

One said, "Flee for your life! Don't stop anywhere or look behind you.

Flee to the high country so that you won't be swept away."

Then Yahweh rained fire and brimstone upon Sodom and Gomorrah.

He destroyed those cities and the land of the plain,

the people, and all that grew there.

But Lot's wife looked back, and she became a pillar of salt.

In the morning, Abraham went to the place

where he had stood before Yahweh.

He looked down at Sodom and Gomorrah, and the land of the plain,
and saw only smoke, rising like ash from a kiln.

GOD HAS GIVEN ME LAUGHTER

Abraham took Sarah and all of his household
and sojourned in Gerar, in the land of Abimelech, the king.
Now Yahweh did for Sarah as He had spoken,
and she conceived and bore a son to Abraham in his old age.
And Abraham called the name of his son Isaac,
and he circumcised his son, Isaac, when he was eight days old
as Yahweh had commanded him.
Abraham was one hundred years old when Isaac, his son, was born.
Sarah said, "God has given me laughter.
Now everyone who hears will laugh for me.

       Who would have said to Abraham,

'Sarah will nurse sons'?
But I have borne a son in his old age."

The child grew and was weaned,
and Abraham made a great feast for his weaning day.
But Sarah saw the son of Hagar the Egyptian playing.
She said to Abraham, "Drive out this slave girl and her son
so that the son shall not share inheritance with my son, Isaac."
Abraham was greatly troubled, but God said to him,
"Do not let it seem evil, this matter of the slave and the boy.
In all that Sarah asks, do as she says.
For it is through her son, Isaac, that your children will be acclaimed.
But the son of the slave woman — a nation will I make of him, too."

Early in the morning, Abraham gave Hagar
some bread and a skin of water,
placing them on her shoulder, and he sent her away with the boy.
She went off and wandered in the wilderness near Beersheba.
And when the water in the skin was gone,
she threw the boy under a bush
and sat at a distance, a bow shot away;
she did not want to see the child die.
And sitting there, she raised up her voice and wept.
But God heard the boy weeping,
and God's messenger called to Hagar and said to her:
"Fear not. God has heard.
Lift up the boy,
and take him by the hand,
for a great nation I will make of him."

Then she saw a well of water and filled the skin and let the boy drink.

26

God was with him as he grew up and dwelled in the wilderness,

and he became a bowman.

He settled in the wilderness in Paran,

and his mother found him a wife from the land of Egypt.

At that time, Abimelech the king said to Abraham,

"God is with you in all that you do.

Swear to me by God that you will deal loyally

with me and the land where you have sojourned."

And Abraham said, "I swear it."

HERE I AM

And now it happened

that God tested Abraham and said to him,

"Abraham!"

And he said, "Here I am."

God said,

"Take your son,

your only one,

whom you love,

Isaac,

and go forth to the land of Moriah,

and offer him as a burnt offering

on one of the mountains

that I will tell you."

Abraham set out early in the morning.

He saddled his donkey,

he took his two serving boys and Isaac, his son,

he split wood for the offering,
and rose and went toward the place that God had told him.

On the third day, Abraham lifted his eyes and saw it.
And he said to the serving boys, "Wait here with the donkey.
The boy and I will go ahead and worship,
and then we will return to you."
Abraham took the wood for the fire
and put it on Isaac, his son.
And in his own hand he took a firestone and a knife.
The two of them went together.

And Isaac said to Abraham his father, "Father!"
Abraham said, "Here I am, my son."
And Isaac said, "Here are the firestone and the wood.
But where is the sheep for the offering?"
Abraham said, "God will see to the sheep for the offering, my son."
The two of them went together.

They came to the place that God had told Abraham,
and he built an altar and laid the wood
and bound Isaac, his son, and placed him on the altar on the wood.
And Abraham reached out his hand
and took the knife to slay his son.
But Yahweh's messenger called to him from heaven and said,
"Abraham! Abraham!"
And he said, "Here I am."
He said, "Do not reach out your hand against your son.
Do not do anything to him,
for now I know
that you fear God —
you have not withheld your son, your only one, from Me."

Then Abraham raised his eyes and saw:
a ram was caught by its horns in the thicket.
He took the ram and offered it as a burnt offering
instead of his son.

Now God's messenger called to Abraham again, saying,
"Because you have done this thing,
have not held back your son, your only one,
I will bless you.
I will make your children a multitude,
like stars in the heavens and sand on the shore.
They shall seize the gates of their enemies
and they shall be a blessing to all the nations of the earth
because you listened to my voice."

A BURIAL TOMB

The span of Sarah's life was one hundred and twenty-seven years,

and she died in Hebron, in the land of Canaan.

Abraham came to lament and mourn for her.

Then he spoke to the Hittites in that land, saying,

"I am a sojourner and settler among you.

Sell me a burial tomb so that I might bury my dead."

The Hittites said to him, "You are exalted by God.

No one will deny you a burial tomb."

But Abraham said to Ephron son of Zohar,

who was sitting with the Hittites at the gate of the town,

"Sell me the cave of Machpelah that belongs to you.

Sell it to me for the silver price."

Ephron answered Abraham, saying,

"The cave and the field near it I give you. Bury your dead."

But Abraham said again in the hearing of the Hittites,

"Sell them to me for the silver price."

And Ephron said, "The land is four hundred silver shekels.

What is that between us? Go and bury your dead."

Abraham weighed out the silver: four hundred silver shekels.

So it was that the cave and the field at Machpelah

and every tree in the field passed to Abraham.

And Abraham buried Sarah, his wife, in the land of Canaan.

REBEKAH CAME WITH HER WATER JAR

Abraham was old, advanced in years

and God had blessed him in all things.

And Abraham said to his servant,

"Put your hand under my thigh, and swear to me by Yahweh,

God of heaven and earth,
that you will not take a wife for my son
from the daughters of the Canaanites, among whom I dwell.
Swear that you instead will go to the land of my birth
to take a wife for my son, for Isaac."
And the servant put his hand under Abraham's thigh
and swore to him.

The servant took ten camels and Abraham's riches in his hand
and traveled to Haran, to the city of Abraham's brother Nahor.
He had the camels kneel down by the water well in the evening,
at the hour when the women came to draw water,
and he said, "God of Abraham, let the woman to whom I say,
'Pray, lower your jar so I can drink,'
say to me, 'Drink, and for your camels, too, I will draw water.'
By this I will know that you have chosen her for my master's son,
for Isaac."
Scarcely had he finished speaking when Rebekah came
with her water jar on her shoulder.
She was beautiful to look at, and no man had known her.
The servant ran to meet her, saying,
"Pray, let me sip a little water from your jar."
She said, "Drink, my lord."
And she lowered her jar and let him drink,
saying, "For your camels, too, I will draw water."
Then she ran again and again to draw water from the well.

The servant watched her.
And when the camels had finished drinking,
he took a gold nose ring and two gold bracelets for her arms,
ten shekels in weight.
He said, "Tell me. Whose daughter are you?

And might we stay the night at your father's house?"
She said to him, "I am the daughter of Bethuel,
who is the son of Nahor.
You are welcome."
Then the man bowed low to Yahweh and said,
"Blessed be Yahweh,
God of Abraham, my master,
who has led me to the house of his kinsmen."

Rebekah ran and told this in her mother's household.
Now, Rebekah had a brother whose name was Laban.
Laban went out to meet the man at the spring.
And when he saw the nose ring and the gold bracelets
on his sister's arms,
Laban ran to him.

And Laban said, "Come, I have made a place for you in the house."
The man came and unbridled the camels and he said,
"I am Abraham's servant. God has blessed my master.
He has given him sheep and cattle, male and female slaves,
camels and asses.
My master's wife, Sarah, bore him a son after he had grown old,
and he has given this son all that he has.
Now, my master made me swear, saying,
'You must go to my clan to take a wife for my son, Isaac.'
And today I came to the spring and then Rebekah came to draw water.
I put the ring in her nose and the bracelets on her arms.
And I bowed low before Yahweh and blessed His name."

And Laban said, "Here is Rebekah before you.
Take her, that she may be a wife for the son of your master
as God has spoken."

Then the servant brought out garments and ornaments

of gold and silver

and gave them to Rebekah,

and gifts for her brother and her mother.

They ate and drank and the man spent the night.

Then they called Rebekah and said to her,

"Will you go with this man?"

And she said, "I will."

And they sent Rebekah off with her maid and blessed her, saying:

> "Our sister, may you become
>
> thousands of myriads.
>
> And may your children
>
> seize the gates of their foes."

Rebekah and her maid mounted camels.

Then the servant took Rebekah and went away.

Isaac had returned from Beer-lahai-roi,

where he was dwelling in the Negev.

He went out walking in the field in the evening.

He lifted his eyes and, here, camels were coming.

Rebekah lifted her eyes and saw Isaac.

And she alighted from her camel and said to the servant,

"Who is that man walking in the field toward us?"

And the servant said, "That is my master, Isaac."

So she took her veil and covered herself.

Then Isaac brought her into the tent of Sarah, his mother,

and he took Rebekah for his wife and loved her.

And Isaac was comforted after his mother's death.

In the ripeness of age

Abraham had taken another wife. Her name was Keturah.
She bore him six sons, and their names were
Zimran and Jokshan and Medan and Midian and Ishbak and Shuah.
But Abraham deeded everything he had to Isaac.
To the others he gave gifts, sending them away from Isaac
to the eastern lands.

The days of Abraham's life were one hundred and seventy-five years.
When he died in the ripeness of age, he was gathered to his kinsmen.
And Isaac and Ishmael, his sons, buried him in the cave of Machpelah
in the field of Ephron, son of Zohar, in Canaan.

And to Ishmael, son of Hagar, the slave girl,
were born twelve sons, twelve chieftains of twelve tribes,
and they dwelled from Havilah to Shur, which faces Egypt.
The days of Ishmael were one hundred and thirty-seven years,
when he died and was gathered to his kinsmen.

Jacob

A CLASHING WAS WITHIN HER

Isaac was born to Abraham,

and he was forty years old when he took Rebekah for a wife.

And Isaac pleaded to Yahweh on Rebekah's behalf, for she was barren.

Yahweh granted his plea, and Rebekah conceived.

But a clashing was within her, and she said,

"Then why me?" and she went to ask Yahweh.

And He said to her:

> "Two nations are in your womb;
>
> two shall come from your body.

But one will be mightier,

    the older a slave to the younger."

And true, when it was time for the birth,

there were twins in her womb.

The first one came out red, like a hairy mantle all over,

and they called his name *Esau:* rough one.

Then his brother came out, his hand grasping Esau's heel,

and they called his name *Jacob:* heel holder.

The boys grew up.

Esau became a hunter, a man of the fields,

and Jacob was a quiet man who stayed in the tents.

Isaac loved Esau for the game he killed,

but Rebekah loved Jacob.

Once when Jacob was cooking a stew, Esau came in

famished.

And Esau said to Jacob, "Let me gulp some red stuff, that red stuff,

for I am famished."

And Jacob said, "Then sell me your firstborn birthright.

Sell it to me now in exchange."

Esau said, "I am almost dead with hunger.

So what good is my birthright to me?"

Jacob said, "Swear to me now."

And Esau swore to him, and he ate bread and boiled red lentils

and sold his birthright.

When Esau was forty years old, he took Judith the Hittite

and Basemath the Hittite for his wives.

But they provoked Isaac and Rebekah and were thorns to them.

I am Esau, your firstborn

When Isaac was old and his eyes had grown dim,
he called Esau, his older son, to him and said, "My son."
And Esau answered, saying, "Here I am."
Isaac said, "I do not know the day when I will die.
So now take up your quiver and your bow, and hunt me some game
and make me food from it, of the kind I love.
Bring it to me, and I will eat
so I may give you my blessing before I die."

Now, Rebekah was listening as Isaac spoke
and she said to Jacob, her son, her favorite,
"Look, I heard your father saying to Esau,
'Bring me some game and make me food
so that I may bless you in Yahweh's presence.'
So now, my son, listen to all that I say:

Go to the flock and bring me two goat kids,
and I will make your father food of the kind he loves.
You shall bring it to him to eat
that he might bless you before he dies."

And Jacob said to Rebekah, his mother,
"But Esau is a hairy man and I am a smooth man.
If my father touches me, he will think me a thief
and I will bring upon myself his curse and not his blessing."
His mother said, "Your curse, my son, will be upon me.
Now, listen and go; bring them to me."

Jacob went and brought the goats to his mother,
and she made food of the kind his father loved.
And she took the garments of Esau, her older son,
and clothed Jacob, her younger son.
With the skins of the goat kids,

she covered his hands and the smooth part of his neck.
Then she placed the food in the hand of Jacob, her son.

He came in to his father and said, "Father!"
Isaac said, "Here I am. Who are you, my son?"
Jacob said to his father, "I am Esau, your firstborn.
Rise. Sit up and eat the game that I killed
so that you might bless me."
His father said, "How did you find it so quickly?"
And Jacob said, "Yahweh, your God, made the animal come."
Then Isaac said to Jacob,
"Move close that I might feel you, whether you are my son Esau
or not."

Isaac felt him, saying,
"The voice is Jacob's, but the hands are Esau's, hairy."
And Isaac said, "Are you my son Esau?"
Jacob said, "I am."
And Isaac said, "Serve me; let me eat the hunted game of my son."
Jacob served it to him and he ate,
and brought him wine and he drank.
Then Isaac, his father, said to him,
"Here, come close and kiss me, my son."
And Jacob came close and kissed him.
Now Isaac smelled his garments and said:

> "The smell of my son is like the smell of a field
> that Yahweh has blessed.
> May nations serve you.
> May tribes bow down before you.
> Be master to your brothers.
> May your brothers bow down to you.
> Those who curse you, cursed.
> Those who bless you, blessed."

And it happened when Isaac had finished blessing Jacob
that Esau came back from the hunt.
And he, too, made food for his father and brought it to him.
He said to his father,
"Rise. Sit up and eat the game I killed
so that you might bless me."
And his father, Isaac, said, "Who are you?"
And he said, "I am your son, your firstborn, Esau."

Then Isaac was seized with a great trembling and he said,
"Who is it, then, who brought me game? I ate everything
and blessed him!
Now blessed he will remain."
When Esau heard his father's words, he cried with bitter crying.
And Isaac said, "Your brother came like a thief
and took away your blessing."
Esau said, "Have you not saved a blessing for me?
Bless me, too, Father!"
Then he lifted his voice and wept.
Isaac, his father, answered, saying to him:

> "You will serve your brother.
> But when you rebel,
> you will break his yoke from your neck."

Now Esau hated Jacob because of the blessing and he said,
"When the time comes for mourning my father,
I will kill my brother."
Rebekah was told of Esau's words, and she sent for Jacob,
her younger son,
and said to him, "Look, your brother, Esau, is consoling himself
by planning to kill you. So now, my son, listen to me.
Arise and flee to my brother in Haran

and stay with him for some days until your brother's anger is gone.
Then I will send for you, to bring you back."

And Rebekah said to Isaac, "I hate my life
because of Esau's Hittite women.
If Jacob also marries a Hittite woman, what good will my life be?"

THE GATE OF HEAVEN

And Isaac sent for Jacob and said to him,
"You must not take a wife from the Hittites of Canaan.
Arise and go to Haran and take a wife from there,
from the daughters of Laban, your mother's brother.
May God bless you and make you many
so that you become an assembly of tribes."

Jacob left Beersheba and set out for Haran.
And when the sun had set, he came to a place
and had to stay the night.
He took one of the stones and put it at his head and lay down there.
And he dreamed.
Here, a stairway was upon the earth and its top reached the sky,
and messengers of God were going up and coming down on it.
And Yahweh was standing over him.
He said, "I am Yahweh,
the God of Abraham and the God of Isaac.
The land where you are, I give it to you and your children.
And they shall be like the dust of the earth.
And you shall burst forth to the east, to the west,
to the north, to the south.
And the clans of the earth shall be blessed through you.

Remember, I am with you.
I will protect you wherever you go and bring you back to this land."

Then Jacob woke from his sleep and said,
"Yahweh is in this place, and I did not know."
And he was afraid and said:

>"How awesome is the house of God!
>It is the gate of heaven."

Then Jacob rose and took the stone he had put at his head
and set it as a pillar and poured oil over it.
The place was called Luz, but Jacob named it *Beth-el:* House of God.
He made a vow, saying, "If Yahweh is with me,
if He protects me on the way I am going
and I return safe to my father's house,
then Yahweh shall be my God.
And this stone that I set as a pillar shall be a house of God."

RACHEL CAME WITH HER FATHER'S SHEEP

Jacob lifted his feet and continued east, to Haran.
And there was a well in the field and sheep lying near it,
and a big stone was on the mouth of the well.
Jacob said to the shepherds, "Do you know Laban, son of Nahor?"
They said, "Yes, we know him,
and Rachel, his daughter, is coming with the sheep."
Jacob said, "Look, it is still bright daylight.
Water the sheep and take them to graze."
The shepherds said, "We cannot until all the herds are gathered.
Then we roll the stone away from the well."

Now Rachel came with her father's sheep.

And when Jacob saw her, he stepped forward

and rolled the stone from the mouth of the well

and watered the sheep of Laban, his mother's brother.

And Jacob kissed Rachel and lifted up his voice and wept.

He told Rachel that he was her father's kinsman,

that he was Rebekah's son.

She ran and told her father.

And it happened, when Laban heard the news,

he ran to Jacob and kissed him and brought him into his house,

saying, "You are my bone and flesh."

Jacob stayed with him for a month's time and Laban said to him,

"Because you are my kinsman, should you serve me for nothing?

Tell me what your wages will be."

Now, Laban had two daughters.

The older was called Leah, and Rachel was the younger,

but Rachel was beautiful to look at

and Jacob loved Rachel.

And he said to Laban, "I will serve you for seven years

for Rachel, your younger daughter."

Laban said, "Better I should give her to you than another man.

Stay with me."

So Jacob served Laban for seven years, and they seemed to him

but a few days in his love for Rachel.

Then Jacob said to Laban, "Come, now give me my wife."

Laban gathered the people of the place and made a feast.

And when evening came, he took Leah, his daughter,

and brought her to Jacob

and Jacob lay with her.

And when morning came, look, she was Leah!

And he said to Laban, "Was it not for Rachel that I served you?

Why have you deceived me?"

Laban said, "It is not done here, to give away the younger

before the firstborn.

Stay with this one for the bridal week,

and if you serve me for another seven years,

you shall have the other one, too.

Then Jacob lay with Rachel as a wife. And he loved her

more than Leah,

and he served Laban for another seven years.

COME, GIVE ME SONS!

Yahweh saw that Leah was hated, so He opened her womb,

but Rachel was barren.

Leah conceived and bore four sons,

and she called their names Reuben, Simeon, Levi, and Judah.

Rachel saw she could bear no children to Jacob

and was jealous of her sister.

She said to Jacob, "Come, give me sons! If you don't, I will die!"

But Jacob's anger flared and he said,

"Can I take the place of God, who has denied you?"

Then Rachel gave him her slave girl Bilhah, saying,

"Lie with her so that she might give me a son."

Jacob lay with Bilhah and she bore two sons.

And Rachel called their names Dan and Naphtali.

Then Leah took her own slave girl Zilpah and gave her to Jacob.
And Zilpah bore Jacob two sons; their names were Gad and Asher.

Leah's son Reuben went out in the fields in the wheat harvest
and he found mandrake plants and brought them to his mother.
But Rachel wanted the mandrakes to make her fertile,
and she said to Leah,
"Jacob can lie with you tonight in return."
Leah agreed and went to meet him in the evening,
and she bore him a son Issachar and another son Zebulun.
Leah said, "Now my husband will love me,
for I have borne him six sons."
And then she bore him a daughter and called her Dinah.

Then God remembered Rachel. He heard her
and opened her womb at last.
And she conceived and bore a son.
She called his name *Joseph:* may God give me another son.

THUS DID JACOB PROSPER

Now, after Rachel bore Joseph, Jacob said to Laban,
"Let me go, that I might return to my home
with my wives and children.
And Laban said, "I have prospered and God has blessed me
because of you.
Name the wages you would like."
Jacob said, "You know that your livestock
has grown to a multitude in my care.
Let me pass through your herds and pick out the dark sheep,

the speckled and spotted goats, and they will be my wages."
And Laban said, "So shall it be."

But that same day, Laban took the dark sheep,
the speckled and spotted goats,
and gave them to his sons.
And he put three days' journey between himself and Jacob.
Then Jacob peeled white strips from poplar and almond
and plane branches
and set them before the goats.

And the sheep he kept apart, facing all the dark-colored
in Laban's flock.
From that time, the goats bore only speckled and spotted goats
for Jacob,
and the ewes only dark sheep.
Thus did Jacob prosper, and he had many flocks.

High in Gilead

Laban's sons said, "Jacob has taken everything of our father's."
And Jacob saw that Laban had turned against him.
Then God said to Jacob,
"Return to the land of your fathers. I will be with you."
Jacob sent for Rachel and Leah, to come to him in the fields,
and said to them,
"You know I served your father with all my strength,
and he has cheated me and changed my wages ten times over.
But God has protected me.
His messenger came to me in a dream and said,
'Jacob!'
And I said, 'Here I am.'
His messenger said, 'I have seen what Laban is doing to you.
Now arise. Go. Leave this land and return
to the land of your fathers.'"
Rachel and Leah said,
"Our father regards us as strangers
now that he has sold us and used all our bride-price for himself.
So here, whatever God has said to you, do!"
Their father, Laban, was shearing the sheep,
and Rachel stole his household gods to take with her.
Jacob did not know.

He lifted his children and his wives onto the camels
and led away all his herds, all his property.
They fled, crossing the Euphrates toward
the high hill country of Gilead.

But Laban took his kinsmen and caught up with them.
He said to Jacob, "What have you done, deceiving me,
driving my daughters like captives of the sword?
I would have sent you off with song, with timbrel and lyre.
And why did you steal my gods?"
Jacob said, "That I did not do.
Wherever you find your gods—that person shall not live."
For Jacob did not know that Rachel had stolen them.
Laban came into Jacob's tent, and Leah's, and into the tent
of the slave girls.
And he went into Rachel's tent.
Rachel had taken the gods and hidden them in the camel cushion.
And she sat upon them, and Laban found nothing.

Then Jacob was angered and said to Laban,
"Twenty years have I served you—
fourteen years for your two daughters and six years for your herds.
The scorching heat ate me up by day and the frost by night,
and sleep never came to my eyes.
You would have sent me away empty-handed.
But the God of my fathers, the God of Abraham and Isaac,
was with me.
He saw my suffering and the toil of my hands."
And Laban said to Jacob,
"The daughters are my daughters, the children are my children,
the animals are my animals.

But I can do nothing.

So come, let us make a covenant."

Jacob took a stone and set it as a pillar.

And he said to his kinsmen, "Gather stones."

Laban said, "This mound is a witness between us this day.

I will not cross over to you past the mound and the pillar.

And you will not cross over them to me."

And Jacob offered sacrifice high in Gilead,

and ate bread with his kinsmen and passed the night on the hill.

WHY DO YOU ASK MY NAME?

In the morning, Laban kissed his grandchildren and his daughters

and blessed them, and turned back to Haran.

Jacob went on his way, sending servants before him

to his brother, Esau.

He commanded them, "Say to my lord Esau, 'I am your servant Jacob.

I sojourned with Laban these twenty years.

And I gained sheep and goats, oxen and donkeys and slaves.

And I send word ahead, my lord, to find favor in your eyes.'"

And the messengers returned to Jacob, saying,

"Your brother, Esau, is coming to meet you,

and four hundred men are with him."

Then Jacob was greatly afraid.

He divided the people into two camps

so that if one were struck the other might escape.

And he said, "God of my father Abraham and my father Isaac,

who has said to me, 'I will bring you back to your land,'

oh, save me now from the wrath of my brother!"

And he collected a gift for Esau: two hundred she-goats
and twenty he-goats,
two hundred ewes and twenty rams, thirty nursing camels
and their young,
forty cows and ten bulls, twenty she-asses and ten he-asses.
And he sent them to Esau as herds before him
so that Esau might look upon him kindly.

Jacob rose that night and took his two wives
and his slave girls and eleven sons
and he crossed over the Jabbok ford.
Jacob took them and brought them across the river,
and he brought across all that he owned.
Jacob was left in the camp alone
and a man came and wrestled with him until dawn.
When he saw that he could not win against Jacob,
the man touched Jacob's hip socket and wrenched it.
And he said to Jacob,
"Let me go, for dawn is breaking."
And Jacob said,
"I will not unless you bless me."
The man said,
"From now on, your name will not be Jacob but *Israel:* God wrestler,
for you have fought with God and men, and won."
And Jacob said,
"Then, what is your name?"
The man said, "Why do you ask my name?" and he blessed him.

Jacob called the name of the place *Peniel:* I have seen God face-to-face
and my life was saved.
Then the sun rose upon Jacob and he was limping on his hip.

And Jacob lifted his eyes and saw that Esau was coming,

and with him were four hundred men.

Jacob divided the children among Leah and Rachel

and the two slave girls,

placing the slave girls and their children first,

then Leah and her children,

and Rachel and Joseph last.

And Jacob went before them and bowed to the ground seven times

until he was next to his brother.

Esau ran to meet him,

and he embraced Jacob and kissed him.

And they wept.

Esau said, "Who are all these with you?"

And Jacob said, "My wives and children, whom God has given me."

The slave girls and Leah and Rachel and their children

bowed down before Esau.

Esau said, "And what about the herds you sent before you?"

Jacob said, "To find favor in your eyes, my lord."

And Esau said, "I have enough, my brother. Keep what is yours."

And Jacob said, "Oh, no, my lord, take this gift from me,

for seeing your face is like seeing the face of God,

and you have received me kindly."

And so he urged Esau, and Esau took it.

Then Esau journeyed onward to Seir,

which was then called Edom.

Jacob said he would follow,

but after Esau left, he turned northward.

And Jacob came in peace to the town of Shechem, which is in Canaan.
He camped facing the town and bought that piece of land
from the sons of Hamor, prince of Shechem.
And he made an altar there and called it
El Elohei Israel: God, God of Israel.

THEY KILLED EVERY MAN

Dinah, the daughter whom Leah had borne to Jacob,
went out among the daughters of the land.
And Shechem, a son of Hamor, saw her and took her
and lay with her by force.
But afterward his heart was with Dinah and he loved her.
And Shechem spoke to Hamor, his father, saying,
"Take me this girl for a wife."

Jacob was with his sons, who had come in from the field.
When they heard that Shechem had abused Dinah,
they were filled with rage.
And then Hamor came and spoke with them, saying,
"Shechem, my son, longs for your daughter.
Pray give her to him as a wife.
Give us your daughters and take our daughters for yourselves.
Settle among us in this land."
And Shechem said, "Name me the bride-price you want
and give her to me."

Jacob's sons answered Shechem and Hamor, his father,
deceitfully, saying,
"We cannot do this thing, to give our sister to a man
who is not circumcised,

for that would be a disgrace to us.
But if you become like us, if every male among you is circumcised,
then we can give our daughters to you and take your daughters
for ourselves."

And Hamor and his son Shechem agreed.
When they came to the gate of their town, they spoke
to the men of their town,
saying, "These men outside come in peace. Let them settle among us.
Let us take their daughters as wives and let us give them our daughters.
But we must be circumcised as they are circumcised. Agree to this."
And it was done.

But on the third day, while the men of the town
were weak and hurting,
two of Jacob's sons, Simeon and Levi, Dinah's brothers,
took their swords and came into the town
and they killed every man.
Hamor and Shechem they killed by the sword,
and they took Dinah from Shechem's house and went out.
Then Jacob's other sons came upon the corpses and looted the town.
The animals in the fields and the wealth in the houses they took,
and the children and women they held captive.
And Jacob said to Simeon and Levi,
"You have stirred up trouble for me,
making me stink among the Canaanites, when we are so few.
They will band together and destroy us."
But his sons said, "Should our sister then be treated like a whore?"

The sons of Jacob

And God said to Jacob,
"Arise and go up to Beth-el and make an altar to the God
who came to you
when you were fleeing from Esau, your brother."
And Jacob said to all who were with him,
"Put away your household gods and purify yourselves,
and let us go to Beth-el."
They gave him their gods and the rings that were in their ears,
and Jacob buried them under a terebinth near Shechem.
Then they moved on.
The terror of God was on the towns they moved through,
and the men did not pursue them.
So Jacob came to Beth-el, in the land of Canaan.
And God appeared to him again and He called his name Israel, saying:

> "Be fruitful and multiply.
> An assembly of nations shall come from you.
> Kings shall come from you.
> And the land I gave to Abraham and Isaac,
> I will give it to you.
> And to your children after you I will give the land."

Then Jacob set up a pillar there and poured oil upon it.

As they journeyed onward from Beth-el, Rachel was giving birth.
She labored hard, and the midwife said to her,
"Do not be afraid. This one, too, is a son for you."
Rachel's life was slipping away. She was dying.
The child's name was called Benjamin.
And Rachel died and was buried on the road to Bethlehem.

Then the sons of Jacob were twelve, and he came to Isaac, his father,
in Hebron,
where Abraham, too, had sojourned.
Isaac's days were one hundred and eighty years.
And when he died in the ripeness of age,
he was gathered to his kinsmen.
Esau and Jacob buried him.

Esau took his wives from the daughters of Canaan, three wives.
And they bore him sons in the land of Canaan.
But Esau took all his household and his livestock and his goods,
and he went away from Jacob, his brother,
for the land could not support them both to dwell together.
And Esau settled high in the hill country of Seir,
and his sons and their sons were chieftains of the clans of Edom.

Joseph

AN ORNAMENTED TUNIC

And so Jacob dwelled in the land of Canaan.
This is the story of Jacob and all his family.

Jacob loved Joseph best among his sons, for Joseph was the child
of his old age,
and Jacob made him an ornamented tunic.
Then his brothers saw that their father loved Joseph best,
and they hated him.
And Joseph dreamed a dream
and told it to his brothers when they were tending the flock, saying,

"Listen to this dream:

We were binding sheaves of wheat in the field,

and look, my sheaf arose, it was standing up,

and your sheaves circled it and bowed down to my sheaf."

His brothers said, "Do you mean to be king, to rule over us?"

And they hated him even more.

But Joseph dreamed another dream

and told it to his father and his brothers, saying,

"Look, the sun and moon and eleven stars were bowing down to me."

His father said, "Are we to come, I and your mother

and your brothers,

to bow down to you to the ground?"

And his father remembered the dream.

Joseph's brothers went to Shechem to graze the flock,

and Israel said to Joseph, "Come, I will send you to them

and the sheep."

And Joseph said, "Here I am."

When Joseph came to Shechem, a man found him

wandering in the field

and showed him the way to his brothers.

They saw him from far away and they plotted to kill him, saying,

"Here he comes, the master dreamer!

Let us kill him and fling him into one of these pits,

and we can say a wild beast has devoured him."

But Reuben said, "Fling him into the pit, but do not shed his blood!"

He meant to come back for Joseph and return him to their father.

So it was when Joseph came to his brothers,

they stripped him of his tunic, the ornamented tunic,

and threw him into the pit.

The pit was empty; there was no water in it.

They sat down to eat bread.

And now a caravan of Ishmaelites was coming,

with camels carrying balm and sweet gum to Egypt.

Judah said, "Why should we kill our brother and cover up his blood?

Let us sell him to the Ishmaelites."

And the Ishmaelites bought Joseph for twenty pieces of silver.

They brought him to Egypt.

Reuben came back to the pit and it was empty.

And he said to his brothers, "The boy is gone, and where can I turn?"

They took Joseph's tunic and dipped it

in the blood of a slaughtered kid.

They brought the bloody thing to their father and said,

"We found this. Is it your son's tunic?"

And Jacob recognized it and said, "It is.

          A wild beast has devoured him!

           Joseph is torn, torn to pieces!"

And Jacob mourned for his son, ripping his clothes in grief.

His sons and daughters tried to console him,

but he would not be comforted.

He said, "No.

I will go to the grave in mourning for my son."

And Jacob wept for him.

POTIPHAR'S WIFE

Joseph was brought down to Egypt.

An Egyptian called Potiphar, a steward in the court of Pharaoh,

bought him from the Ishmaelites,

and he put Joseph in charge of the house.

Then Yahweh blessed the house for Joseph's sake, and the fields.

Joseph was beautiful to look at,

and it happened that Potiphar's wife

raised her eyes to him and said, "Lie here with me."

But Joseph refused, saying, "All that your husband has

he has placed in my hands.

How could I do this evil and offend God?"

Day after day, Potiphar's wife asked him again,

and he would not listen to her.

And then one day when there were no other men in the house,

she seized Joseph by his garment,

and he wrenched away and left it in her hand.

She kept his garment with her until his master returned.

And she spoke to him, saying, "The Hebrew slave you brought us

came in to me, to play with me.

And when I called out in a loud voice, he left his garment and fled.

See it there."

And then his master's anger flared at Joseph.

He took Joseph and put him in the prison house,

in the place where the king's prisoners were kept.

Joseph was in the prison house

and the jailer saw that God was with him

and he put Joseph in charge of the prisoners.

And Yahweh gave Joseph success in all that he did.

THE KING'S CUP BEARER AND HIS BAKER

And it happened that the king's cup bearer and his baker

offended the king and were locked in the prison house,

under Joseph's care.

And the two of them dreamed a dream on a single night,
each his own dream, each with its own meaning.
In the morning, Joseph asked them why they were downcast.
And they said, "We dreamed dreams, and there is no one
to tell their meanings."
Joseph said, "Are not meanings from God?
Pray, tell me the dreams."

The cup bearer said, "In my dream, there was a vine
and three tendrils on it.
They were barely budding, and then a flower ripened into grapes.
Now Pharaoh's cup was in my hand.
I picked the grapes and squeezed them and gave the cup to Pharaoh."
Joseph said, "This is the meaning:
The three tendrils are three days.
In three days, Pharaoh will release you
and you will give him his cup again.
Now, remember me when it goes well for you,
and say my name to Pharaoh
and bring me out of this place.
For I was stolen from the land of the Hebrews,
and here, too, I have done nothing
that I should be put in the pit."

And the baker said to Joseph,
"In my dream, there were three baskets on my head
and, in the top one, breads for Pharaoh,
and birds were eating them from the basket."
Joseph said, "This is the meaning:
The three baskets are three days.
In three days, Pharaoh will take you from here
and hang you from a tree, and the birds will eat your flesh."

And on the third day, Pharaoh's birthday,
Pharaoh released the cup bearer and put the cup in his hand,
and the baker he hanged, as Joseph had said.
But the cup bearer did not remember Joseph.
No, he forgot him.

SEVEN COWS WERE COMING

After two years, Pharaoh dreamed
that out of the Nile seven cows were coming, fat and sleek,
and behind them were seven more cows, thin and scrawny.
They stood in the reeds on the banks of the Nile.
And the thin scrawny cows ate up the seven fat cows.
Pharaoh fell asleep and dreamed again.
And here, on one stalk seven ears of grain were growing,
fat and golden,
and behind them were seven more ears, thin and blasted by wind.
And the thin, wind-blasted ears ate up the seven fat ears.
Then Pharaoh awoke and saw that it was a dream.

Pharaoh was fearful. His heart was beating hard.
He sent for all of Egypt's sorcerers and wise men
to tell him the meaning,
but none could say.
And then the cup bearer at last remembered Joseph.
He said to Pharaoh, "When I was in the prison house,
your baker and I dreamed dreams on a single night.
And there was with us a Hebrew slave
and he told their meanings, and so it came to pass:
I was returned to you as cup bearer, and the other was hanged."

And Pharaoh sent for Joseph.

He was brought from the prison house.

Joseph cut his hair and changed his garments

and came before Pharaoh.

And Pharaoh said to him,

"I have heard that you can tell the meaning of a dream."

And Joseph said to Pharaoh,

"Not I. It is God."

Then Pharaoh told Joseph his two dreams, saying,

"The seven thin cows were foul.

I have not seen anything like them in all of Egypt.

And the ears of grain, too."

And Joseph said to Pharaoh,

"Pharaoh's two dreams are one.

What God is about to do, He has told Pharaoh.

The seven fat cows and the seven fat ears

are seven years of abundance.

And the seven foul cows and the seven shriveled ears

are seven years of famine.

The famine will follow the abundance

and devour the land."

And Joseph said, "Let Pharaoh appoint a man,

an overseer to collect the grain in the time of abundance

and store it as a reserve in the time of famine

so the land will not perish."

And Pharaoh said to Joseph,

"Since God has made you know all this,

you will be my overseer.

And I will put you in charge of all Egypt.

I alone will be greater than you."

Then he removed his ring from his hand and put it on Joseph's hand.

He clothed him in fine linen and put a golden collar around his neck.
And Pharaoh gave him an Egyptian woman, Asenath, for a wife.
And Joseph went out through the land of Egypt.
Joseph was thirty years old when he stood before Pharaoh,
king of Egypt.

Pharaoh's dreams came to pass.
In the time of abundance, Joseph collected grain
like the sand of the sea,
so much that they had to stop counting, for it was beyond measure.
Two sons were born to him:
Manasseh: God has freed me from my hardship
and *Ephraim:* God has made me abundant in the land of my affliction.

Then the seven years of abundance came to an end,
and the seven years of famine began.
There was famine in all the lands, but in Egypt there was grain.
And people came to Egypt, to Joseph, for grain.

BREAD IN EGYPT

Jacob saw that there was bread in Egypt.
He said to his sons, "Why do you keep looking at each other?"
And he said, "Go down to Egypt and buy grain
so that we may live and not die."
So Joseph's brothers took silver and went down,
but Jacob would not send Benjamin
for fear that harm might come to him.
Joseph's brothers came to Joseph and bowed down to him,
their faces to the ground.

And Joseph saw his brothers.

He recognized them but spoke harshly as if they were strangers.

He said, "Where do you come from?"

They said, "From the land of Canaan, to buy grain."

His brothers did not recognize him.

And Joseph saw again the dreams he had dreamed about them.

He said to them, "You are spies!"

They said to him, "No, my lord. We are honest.

We are twelve sons of a single man.

One is no more, and the youngest is with our father now."

Joseph said, "By this shall I test you:

one of you must remain here,

and the rest go bring your youngest brother back to me."

They prepared to do so, saying to each other,

"We are being punished because of what we did to Joseph.

We saw his terror.

He pleaded with us to save him, and we did not listen."

Then Reuben said, "Didn't I say to you, 'Do no wrong to the boy'?

Now we will pay for the spilling of his blood."

They did not know that Joseph understood,

for an interpreter was with them.

Joseph went away from his brothers and wept.

When he was able to return, he took Simeon

and tied him up and kept him.

And Joseph gave orders to fill his brothers' packs with grain

and put back the silver they had brought.

And he gave them food for the journey.

They came home to Jacob, their father, in the land of Canaan,
and they told him all that had happened to them, saying,
"The man called us spies.
He took Simeon and kept him
and said we were to bring back Benjamin
to show that we were honest."
And they emptied their bags of grain
and saw that each one's silver was in his pack.
And they trembled with fear.

Jacob, their father, said to them,
"Joseph is no more and Simeon is no more,
and now you would take Benjamin!
Do you mean to torture me?"
Reuben said to his father, "You may kill my two sons
if I don't bring him back."
And Jacob said,
"No, my son shall not go down with you.
For his brother is dead, and he alone is left.
And if harm should come to him,
my life will be ended."

BENJAMIN'S PORTION

But the famine was severe in the land.
And so when they had finished the grain
they had brought from Egypt,
Jacob said, "Return. Buy us some grain."
Judah said to his father, "But the man told us,
'You shall not see my face unless your brother is with you.'"

And Israel said, "Why did you do this to me?
Why did you tell the man you had another brother?"
They said, "The man asked."

And Judah said to Israel, his father,
"Send the boy with me and we will go,
so that we may live and not die.
I will be responsible.
If I do not bring him back to you, you may hold me guilty forever."
And Israel said, "Do this, then:
Take some balm and honey, some sweet gum and almonds
for a tribute,
and double the silver take in your hand.
Take your brother.
Return to the man, and may God give you mercy before the man."

Joseph's brothers went down to Egypt and stood before him.
And Joseph saw Benjamin with them and said to the one
who was his servant,
"Bring the men to my house and slaughter an animal
so that we might eat together at noon."
And when Joseph came into the house,
his brothers brought him the tribute that was in their hand
and bowed down to him, to the ground.
And he asked how they were
and if their father was well, if he was still alive.
Then Joseph raised his eyes and saw Benjamin, his brother,
his mother's son.
And he said, "This must be your youngest brother,
the one you spoke to me about."
And he said to Benjamin, "May God be gracious to you, my boy."

And Joseph left,

for he was overcome with feeling for his brother.

And he went into a room and wept alone.

He washed his face and came out and said, "Serve bread!"

And they were seated with him, the firstborn according to his rank

and the youngest according to his rank.

And food was passed to them,

but Benjamin's portion was five times more than the others.

THE SILVER GOBLET

And Joseph said to his servant,

"Fill the men's sacks with grain and put back their silver in them.

And my goblet, the silver goblet, put it in the youngest one's sack."

At daybreak the men set off on their donkeys.

They were just outside the city, they had not gone far,

when Joseph said to his servant, "Go after them and say,

'Why have you stolen my master's goblet?'"

His servant caught up with them and said to them these words.

The men said, "We would not steal from him."

The men put their sacks on the ground and the servant searched,

and here, the goblet was in Benjamin's sack.

Then the men ripped their clothes as if someone had died,

and they returned to Joseph's house

and threw themselves on the ground before him.

And Joseph said, "The man in whose hand the goblet was found,

he shall be my slave."

And Judah came closer to him and said,

"Please, my lord, our father is old and this one, Benjamin,

is the child of his old age.

His brother being dead, he is the only one left of his mother.

If we return and the boy is not with us,
my father would go in mourning to the grave.
Take me instead. For how else could I face my father?"

I AM JOSEPH, YOUR BROTHER

Then Joseph could no longer restrain himself,
and he called out to his servants, "Go now!"
And he made himself known to his brothers,
raising his voice in weeping.
And Joseph said to his brothers,
"I am Joseph."
His brothers were overcome. They could not speak.

Joseph said to his brothers, "Pray, come close to me."
They came close and he said,
"I am Joseph, your brother, whom you sold into Egypt.
Do not reproach yourselves that you sold me here.
It was to save life that God sent me on before you,
to preserve you in the time of famine.
God brought me to Pharaoh and made me ruler
over the land of Egypt.
Surely you can see, and my brother Benjamin can see,
that it is I who am speaking to you.
Now you must return to our father and bring him here.
Say to him, 'Thus says Joseph: Come down to me.
You shall dwell near me in Goshen,
you and your sons and the sons of your sons,
your sheep and oxen and all that is yours.'
Hurry and bring our father to me."

And Joseph fell upon Benjamin's neck and wept,

and Benjamin wept upon his neck.

Joseph kissed all his brothers and wept upon them,

and at last his brothers spoke with him.

Then Joseph sent his brothers off with wagons and silver and clothing,

and to Benjamin he gave ten times more.

And his brothers went up from Egypt and came to their father, Jacob,

in the land of Canaan.

And they said to him,

"Joseph is alive! He is the ruler of all Egypt."

Jacob's heart froze; he did not believe them.

But when he saw the wagons and all that Joseph had given them,

Israel came back to himself and he said,

"My son Joseph is alive! Let me go to him before I die!"

NOW I CAN DIE

Israel set out with all that was his, and he came to Beersheba,

where he gave sacrifices to the God of his father Isaac.

And God called to Israel in visions of the night and said,

"Jacob! Jacob!"

And Jacob said, "Here I am."

And God said, "I am God, the God of your father.

Do not be afraid to go down to Egypt,

for a great nation will I make of you there.

I will go down with you to Egypt and I will bring you up again,

and when you die, Joseph's hand will close your eyes."

Then Jacob left Beersheba

with his sons and the sons of his sons,

his daughters and the daughters of his sons,
and all that they had gained in the land of Canaan.
In the wagons Joseph had given them
they came into Egypt.
And with Joseph and his two sons born to him in Egypt,
the people in Jacob's family were seventy.

When Jacob came to Goshen,
Joseph harnessed his chariot and went to meet Israel, his father.
He saw his father and fell on his neck and wept for a long time.
Israel said to Joseph, "Now that I have seen your face
and I know you are still alive, now I can die."

Then Joseph brought Jacob, his father, to stand before Pharaoh,
and Jacob blessed Pharaoh.
Pharaoh said to Jacob, "How many are the years of your life?"
And Jacob said,
"One hundred and thirty are my years on the earth.
Few and painful have they been,
and they have not reached the years of my fathers."
And Jacob blessed Pharaoh again and went away.

Israel lived seventeen years in Goshen, in the land of Egypt,
and the years of his life were one hundred and forty-seven.
And when the time came for Israel to die,
he called his son Joseph and said to him,
"If I have found favor in your eyes,
put your hand under my thigh and swear to me.
Act toward me with steadfast love.
Pray, do not bury me in Egypt!
When I lie down with my fathers,
carry me out of Egypt and bury me in their burial place."

Joseph said, "I will do what you ask."

But Israel said, "Swear to me!"

So Joseph swore it.

AN ASSEMBLY OF TRIBES

Now it happened that Jacob became ill.

Someone told Joseph and he came with his sons,

Manasseh and Ephraim.

Israel gathered his strength and sat up.

And he said to Joseph,

"God appeared to me at Beth-el, in the land of Canaan.

He blessed me and He said to me,

'I will make you fruitful and you will be many.

You will be an assembly of tribes.

And I will give this land to your children, as a holding for all time.'

So now bring your sons to me so that I may bless them."

Joseph brought his two sons close to Jacob,

and Jacob embraced them and said to Joseph,

"I never thought I would see your face again,

and here God has let me see your children also."

Israel's eyes were dim with age; he was almost blind.

He stretched out his right hand and put it on the head of Ephraim,

who was younger,

and his left hand on Manasseh's head.

He crossed his arms, though Manasseh was the firstborn,

and blessed them, saying:

> "The God in whose presence walked my fathers,
>
> Abraham and Isaac,
>
> the God who redeemed me from evil,

the God who cared for me
from the day of my birth until this day,
bless these sons.
That in them may be called my name
and the name of my fathers,
Abraham and Isaac.
And let them become multitudes upon the earth."

Now, when Joseph saw that his father had put his right hand
on Ephraim's head, he thought it was wrong.
And he said to his father, "No. The other one, Manasseh,
is the firstborn.
Put your right hand on him."

And his father refused, saying, "I know, my son, I know—
he, too, will be a people. He, too, will be great,
yet his younger brother will be greater, and his sons will be nations."
Thus did Jacob put Ephraim before Manasseh.
And he said to Joseph, "I am about to die,
but God will be with you, and He will bring you back
to the land of your fathers."

AND JOSEPH COMFORTED HIS BROTHERS

Then Jacob called all his sons to him and blessed them.
And he said, "I am now to be gathered to my kinsmen.
Bury me with my fathers in the cave of Machpelah
in the field of Ephron, son of Zohar, in Canaan,
the field that Abraham bought as a burial holding."
When Jacob had finished commanding his sons,
he gathered up his feet in the bed and breathed no more.

Joseph flung himself on his father's face
and wept over him and kissed him.
Then Joseph told the physicians to embalm his father.
When the days for weeping had passed,
Joseph spoke to Pharaoh, saying,
"Pray, let me go to Canaan to bury my father
as he commanded me."
And Pharaoh said, "Go and bury your father."

And Joseph went up to Canaan with his household,
and Joseph's brothers and their households.
Only the sheep and oxen and the little children were left behind.
Chariots and horsemen accompanied them.

They came across the Jordan to Canaan,
and for seven days again they wept for Jacob.

Then Jacob's sons did as he had commanded.
They buried him in the cave of Machpelah
in the field of Ephron, son of Zohar, in Canaan,
the field that Abraham bought as a burial holding.
And they returned to Egypt.

Joseph's brothers said to each other, "Now that our father is dead,
Joseph might take revenge for the crime we did to him."
So they went to him, saying,
"Before his death, your father asked you to forgive your brothers
for the crime they did to you.
So now pray forgive the servants of your father's God."
Joseph wept as they spoke to him.
And his brothers came and flung themselves before him and said,
"Here we are, your slaves."

But Joseph said, "Do not be afraid. Am I instead of God?
Besides, though you meant me evil, God meant it for good,
so that I could help many people to survive."
And Joseph comforted his brothers.

Joseph dwelled in Egypt, he and his father's household.
He lived a hundred and ten years
and saw the third generation of sons from his sons
Ephraim and Manassah.
And Joseph said to his brothers,
"I am about to die, but God will come to you
and take you from this land
to the land He promised to Abraham, to Isaac, and to Jacob."
And Joseph made his brothers swear to him, saying,
"When God comes to you, bring my bones up from here."
And Joseph died, one hundred and ten years old.
They embalmed him and they put him in a coffin in Egypt.

EXODUS

שמות

In Egypt

A NEW KING

These are the names of the sons of Israel
who came to Egypt with Jacob, each with his household:
Reuben, Simeon, Levi, and Judah;
Issachar and Zebulun;
Dan and Naphtali; Gad and Asher; and Benjamin.
And Joseph was already in Egypt.
The people were twelve tribes, seventy in number.

Now Joseph died, and all his brothers, and all that generation.
But the Israelites were fruitful;
they multiplied and increased greatly,
and the land was filled with them.

A new king arose over Egypt, who had not known Joseph,
and he said to his people,
"Look, the children of the sons of Israel are too many for us.
We must deal with them shrewdly
so that they do not increase even more.
If a war breaks out, they could join our enemies
and make war upon us."
So the Egyptians forced the Israelites into labor,
with masters to oversee them.
And they built cities for Pharaoh — Pithom and Rameses.
The Israelites were afflicted, but still they multiplied
and the Egyptians hated and feared them more.
They made the Israelites do crushing labor, with mortar and bricks.

And the king of Egypt spoke to the midwives of the Hebrews —
their names were Shiphrah and Puah.
He said, "When you deliver a Hebrew woman,
if the child is a boy, kill him, but if it is a girl, she may live."
The midwives feared God and did not do what the king said.
They let all the children live.
Then the king summoned the midwives, saying,
"Why have you let the boys live?"
And the midwives said to Pharaoh,
"The Hebrew women are not like the Egyptian women.
They are strong.
Before the midwife can come to them, they have given birth!"
God rewarded the midwives.
And the people multiplied and grew great.

Then Pharaoh commanded the Egyptians, saying,
"Every Hebrew boy that is born, you must throw him into the Nile.
But let every girl live."

She called his name Moses

A man from the tribe of Levi took a Levite daughter for a wife,
and the woman conceived and bore a son.
When she saw the child and he was goodly,
she hid him for three months.
And when she could no longer hide him,
she took a little ark of papyrus,
and caulked it with resin,
and placed the child in it,
and put it in the reeds by the shore of the Nile.
The child's sister stood near to know that he was safe.

Then Pharaoh's daughter came down to bathe in the Nile
while her maidens walked along the river.
And she saw the little ark among the reeds and took it.
And she opened it and saw a child weeping.

She took pity on him and said, "I know this is a Hebrew child."
Then his sister said to Pharaoh's daughter,
"Shall I find you a Hebrew woman to nurse him?"
And Pharaoh's daughter agreed.
The girl went to her own mother, the child's mother,
and the woman took him and nursed him
until he was old enough for weaning.
Then the woman gave him to Pharaoh's daughter
and he became her son
and she called his name *Moses,* for she had pulled him from the water.

Years passed and Moses grew up and went out among his people.
And he saw their enslavement and their pain.
An Egyptian was beating a Hebrew man.
Moses turned to see that no one was watching,
and he struck down the Egyptian and buried him in the sand.
The next day, again he went out,
and two Egyptian men were fighting with each other.
He said to the guilty one, "Why do you strike your kinsman?"
The Egyptian said, "Who made you a judge over us?
Do you mean to kill me as you did the other one?"
Moses was frightened and thought, "Then my act is known!"
And Pharaoh heard of it and sought to kill Moses.

Moses fled to the land of Midian, far from Pharaoh,
and he sat beside a well.
Now, the priest of Midian had seven daughters,
and they came to the well to draw water for their father's sheep.
Shepherds drove them off,
but Moses rose up and rescued them and drew water for their flock.
When they returned to their father, they said,
"An Egyptian man rescued us from the shepherds."

Their father said, "So where is he?
Call him now so that he may eat bread with us."
Then Moses came and dwelled with the man,
and he gave Moses his daughter Zipporah for a wife.
And she bore a son and Moses called his name
Gershom: sojourner,
saying, "A sojourner I have been in a foreign land."

Many years later, the king of Egypt died.
The Israelites moaned in pain at their bondage; they cried out to God.
And God heard their voices, and He remembered His covenant
with Abraham, with Isaac, and with Jacob.
God saw the Israelites, and He knew.

THE BURNING BUSH

Moses was herding the flock of his father-in-law, the priest of Midian,
and he led the flock far into the wilderness —
he came to the mountain of God.
And God's messenger appeared to him in a fire in a desert bush.
Moses saw, and here, the bush was burning with fire
but the bush was not consumed.
He came closer
and God called to him from the burning bush, "Moses, Moses!"
He said, "Here I am."
And God said, "Come no closer!
Take your sandals from your feet,
for the place where you stand, it is holy ground."
And God said, "I am the God of your fathers,
the God of Abraham, Isaac, and Jacob."
Moses hid his face, for he was afraid to look at God.

Now Yahweh said, "I have seen the affliction of My people in Egypt,

and I know their pain.

And I have come to rescue them from their slave masters

and to take them out of Egypt to a land flowing

with milk and honey —

to the place of the Canaanite and the Hittite,

of the Amorite and the Perizzite, of the Hivite and the Jebusite.

And now, go,

for I am sending you to Pharaoh to bring My people out of Egypt!"

And Moses said to God,

"Who am I to go to Pharaoh, to bring the Israelites out of Egypt?"

God said, "I will be with you.

And when you bring the people out of Egypt,

you will worship God at this mountain."

Moses said, "What shall I say if the Israelites ask me Your name?"

And God said to Moses,

"Tell them *Eyeh-Asher-Eyeh:* I Am What I Will Be.

Say '*Eyeh* has sent me to you.

And it shall

be My name forever.'

"Go, gather the elders of Israel, and they will listen to your voice.

And they will come with you to the king of Egypt,

and together you will say to him,

'Yahweh, the God of the Hebrews, appeared to us.

Now let us go three days into the wilderness

so that we may make offerings and celebrate our God.'

But the king of Egypt will not let you go.

And I will send forth My hand and strike Egypt with all My wonders.

After that he will let you go."

THE STAFF OF GOD

Moses answered and said to Him,

"The people will not believe me, for they will say,

'Yahweh did not appear to you.'"

Then Yahweh said, "What is that in your hand?"

Moses said, "A staff."

And Yahweh said, "Throw it to the ground!"

Moses threw it to the ground and it became a snake,

and he fled from it.

Yahweh said, "Put out your hand and grasp its tail."

Moses put out his hand and grasped it, and the

snake became a staff again.

And Yahweh said, "Put your hand on your naked chest."

Moses did and here, when he brought his hand out,

it was dead white.

Yahweh said, "Put it back on your chest."

Moses did and now his hand was like his own flesh again.

And Yahweh said, "If they do not listen to the voice

of these signs —

either the first one or the second one —

then take water from the Nile and pour it on dry land

and it will become blood."

Moses said to Yahweh,

"Please, my God, I am not a man of words,

not even now that You have spoken to Your servant,

for I am slow of speech and heavy of tongue."

And Yahweh said to him,

"Who gave a mouth to human beings?

Who makes someone mute or deaf or sighted or blind?

Is it not I, Yahweh?

And now, go!
I will be with your mouth. I will tell you what to say."

And Moses said, "Please, my God, send someone else."
Then God's anger blazed at Moses, and He said,
"There is Aaron the Levite, your brother.
Here, he is coming to meet you!
He can speak for you and you will be like a god for him.
And this staff—take it in your hand to do the signs."

Moses went and returned to his father-in-law and said,
"Let me return to my brothers in Egypt, to see if they are still alive."
And his father-in-law said, "Go in peace."
And Yahweh said to Moses in Midian,
"Go, return to Egypt, for all the men who sought you are dead."
Then Moses took his wife and son and mounted them on a donkey,
and he took the staff of God in his hand.
And Yahweh said to him, "The signs that I have given to you,
you must do before Pharaoh.
But I will harden his heart so that he will not let the people go.
Tell Pharaoh that Yahweh says this:
'My son, My firstborn, is Israel.'
And tell Pharaoh further:
'If you will not free him so that he can worship Me,
then I will kill your own son, your firstborn.'"

At a night encampment on the way,
Yahweh waited for Moses and tried to kill him.
But his wife, Zipporah, circumcised her son
and protected Moses with the blood, saying,
"You are a bridegroom of blood to me!"
And Yahweh let him go.

Then Yahweh went to Aaron and said to him,

"Go to the wilderness to meet Moses."

And Aaron went and met Moses on the mountain of God

and kissed him.

Moses told Aaron all that Yahweh had said

and the signs He had given him.

Then Moses and Aaron gathered the elders of the Israelites,

and Aaron said the words that Yahweh had spoken to Moses

and he did the signs before their eyes.

Then the people knew that Yahweh had seen

the affliction of the Israelites,

and they bowed low before Him.

QUOTA OF BRICKS

Now Moses and Aaron went to Pharaoh and they said,

"Yahweh, the God of Israel, commands:

'Set free My people so that they can worship Me in the wilderness.'"

But Pharaoh said, "Who is Yahweh that I should listen to His voice?

I do not know Yahweh, and I will not set Israel free.

Go back to your work!"

And that day Pharaoh commanded the slave drivers, saying,

"You are no longer to give the people straw to make bricks.

Let them go and pick straw stubble themselves.

But do not deduct from the number of bricks—

they must make as many bricks as yesterday and the day before,

for they are lazy.

They cry out, saying they will worship their God!

If their work is heavier, they will not listen to lying words."

Then the people spread out all through Egypt, picking straw stubble.
The slave drivers worked them hard.
And the Hebrew foremen, whom the slave drivers had set over them,
were beaten when they could not complete the task.
The foremen came to Pharaoh, asking for straw
to make the quota of bricks.
But he said, "Lazy, you are lazy!
That is why you say, 'Let us go worship our god.'
No straw will be given to you. Now go!"

Moses and Aaron were waiting when the foremen
came out from Pharaoh.
And the foremen said to them, "May God see you and punish you!
You have made us vile in their eyes and put a sword into their hands
to kill us!"
Then Moses returned to Yahweh and said,
"Why did You send me?
Since I came to Pharaoh to speak in Your name,
he has wounded Your people and You have not delivered them."

And Yahweh said to Moses,
"You will see what I will do to Pharaoh.
I will multiply My signs and wonders in the land of Egypt.
Pharaoh will not listen to you, so I will lift My hand against Egypt,
and I will bring out My armies, My people the Israelites,
from the land of Egypt, with acts of vengeance."

BLOOD WAS EVERYWHERE

Pharaoh was walking to the Nile,
and Moses and Aaron met him on the shore of the Nile.

Moses took in his hand the staff that changed into a snake
and he said to Pharaoh, "Thus says Yahweh:
'Set free My people so they may worship Me in the wilderness!
But you have not listened until now.
By this shall you know that I am Yahweh!'"
Then Aaron took the staff and struck the water in the Nile
before the eyes of Pharaoh and his servants.
And all the water in the Nile turned to blood.
The fish in the Nile died and the Nile stank
and blood was in the ponds and in the rivers,
in the stone containers and the wooden ones.
The people could not drink or find water,
and blood was everywhere in the land of Egypt.
Then Pharaoh called his sorcerers—
they, too, made blood with their spells.
And Pharaoh's heart was hardened.

When seven days had passed,
Moses and Aaron went again
to Pharaoh
and Moses said, "Yahweh says thus:
'Set free My people so
they may worship Me.'"
Then Aaron stretched the staff
over the water of the Nile
and frogs swarmed out and
covered the land of Egypt.

The frogs came into Pharaoh's house and
into his bedroom and upon his couch,
into the houses of the people, into their ovens
and their kneading bowls.
And they came on all the people.
Then Pharaoh called his sorcerers and they, too,
made frogs cover Egypt.

And Pharaoh said to Moses and Aaron,
"Ask your god, Yahweh, to take away the frogs.
And I will set the people free, that they might worship Him."
Moses said to Pharaoh,
"So that you will know there is none like Yahweh,
tomorrow the frogs will retreat back from you.
Only in the Nile will they remain."
Then the frogs died from the houses, the courtyards, and the fields.
The people piled them up in heaps, and the land stank.
But when Pharaoh saw that the frogs had retreated,
his heart hardened again, as Yahweh had spoken.

Then Yahweh said to Moses, "Tell Aaron,
'Hold out your staff and strike the dust of the earth
and it will turn to lice in the land of Egypt.'"
And Aaron did and lice were on the people and the animals in Egypt.
Now the sorcerers tried to bring out the lice, but they could not.
They said to Pharaoh, "It is the finger of God."
But Pharaoh did not listen.
In the morning, Moses waited for Pharaoh;
here, he was walking to the Nile.
And he said to Pharaoh, "Thus says Yahweh:
'Set free My people so they may worship Me.
And if you do not set My people free,

I will loose upon Egypt a swarm of insects, in the houses
and in the soil.
But in Goshen where My people, the Israelites, live,
no swarm will be there
so you will know that I am Yahweh.'"
And Egypt was ravaged by the swarm of insects
but Goshen was spared.

Then Pharaoh sent for Moses and Aaron and said,
"I will set you free that you might worship God in the wilderness.
Only you must not go far.
Plead for me to Yahweh!"
Then Moses left Pharaoh and pleaded for him,
and the swarm left Egypt.
But still Pharaoh would not let the people go.

ALL WAS STRUCK AND BROKEN

Yahweh said to Moses,
"You must say to Pharaoh, 'If you will not let My people go,
My hand will be on your animals in the field—
your horses, your donkeys, your cattle, your sheep.
I will strike them with a heavy plague.
But no animals of the Israelites will die.'"
It came to pass, just so, but still Pharaoh did not set the people free.

And Yahweh said to Moses and Aaron,
"Take soot from the kiln, and let Moses throw it up before Pharaoh
and it will become dust in the land of Egypt
and a rash of burning boils on people and animals."
Moses did thus.

The sorcerers could not stand before Moses
because the boils were upon them.
But Yahweh hardened Pharaoh's heart.

Yahweh said to Moses,
"Early in the morning, go before Pharaoh and say to him,
'I could have stretched out My hand and struck you down
and you would have vanished.
But I let you live, so that you would know My power,
and so that My name would be known in all the earth.'"
Moses said thus,
then he stretched his staff up into the sky and thunder boomed.
Yahweh rained hail and fire on the land of Egypt.
The livestock and the people, the trees and grasses in the fields—
all was struck and broken.
But there was no hail in Goshen, where the Israelites lived.

Pharaoh sent for Moses and Aaron and said to them,
"This time I have done wrong.
Stop the hail and thunder! Plead for me!"
Then Moses went outside the city and spread out his hands
to Yahweh.
The thunder ceased and the hail no longer fell.
But Pharaoh again began to do wrong, as Yahweh had spoken.

And Yahweh said to Moses,
"Go to Pharaoh!
For I have made his heart hard and stubborn,
so that I might send loose My signs in the land
and so that you may tell your son and your son's son
how I have played with Egypt."
Then Moses and Aaron went to Pharaoh and said to him,

"Thus says Yahweh:
'How long will you refuse to humble yourself before Me?
Set free My people, or I will bring a horde of locusts into your land,
as your father and your father's fathers have not seen until this day.'"

And Moses and Aaron left, and Pharaoh's servants said to him,
"Let the men go to worship their god!
Do you not yet know that Egypt is lost?"

Moses and Aaron were called back
and Pharaoh said to them, "Who is going?"
And Moses said, "All of us will go, for it is a festival of God."
But Pharaoh said, "No, only the men."
And he drove Moses and Aaron from his presence.

DARKNESS IN EGYPT

Now Moses stretched out his staff over the land of Egypt,
and Yahweh sent an east wind all that day and night.
When it was morning, the locusts came.
They covered Egypt, and the ground went dark.
All that was green, the locusts consumed—every plant left by the hail.

Pharaoh called back Moses and Aaron and said,
"I stand guilty before your god. Only remove this death from me!"
Then Moses pleaded to Yahweh.
And Yahweh shifted the wind to the west,
and it lifted the locusts and flew them into the Sea of Reeds.
Not one locust remained in Egypt.
But Yahweh hardened Pharaoh's heart
and he did not set the people free.

Then Yahweh said to Moses,

"Stretch out your arm to the sky and let there be darkness in Egypt."

And Moses stretched out his arm, and dark covered everything.

For three days, no one could rise from where they were,

but the Israelites had light in their houses.

Pharaoh said to Moses, "Go, worship Yahweh!

Your children, too, may go.

Only your sheep and cattle leave behind."

But Moses said, "We will take our flocks and herds

for burnt offerings and to sacrifice to God—not a hoof will remain."

And again Yahweh hardened Pharaoh's heart and he said to Moses,

"Go away from me! Do not see my face again,

for on the day you see my face, you will die!"

And Moses said, "You are right. I will not see your face again."

A Passover offering

Yahweh said to Moses,
"I will bring one last plague upon Pharaoh and upon Egypt.
You must stand again before Pharaoh and he will set you free.
Now tell the Israelites, the men and the women,
to ask their neighbors for ornaments of silver and gold."
Yahweh granted the people favor in the eyes of the Egyptians,
and Moses was admired, too, in the land of Egypt.
And the ornaments were given.

Then Moses said to Pharaoh, "Thus says Yahweh:
'At midnight I will go out among the Egyptians
and every firstborn in the land of Egypt will die —
from the firstborn of Pharaoh on his throne
to the firstborn of the slave girl behind the millstones
and all the firstborn of the cattle.
And there will be a great crying through the land of Egypt,
such as has never been nor ever will be again.
But not a dog will snarl or lunge at the Israelites —
and then you will know how I separate My people from Egypt.'"
Then hot anger rose in Moses and he went away from Pharaoh.

And Yahweh said to Moses and Aaron in the land of Egypt,
"This new moon shall be the beginning of the year for you.
Speak to the Israelites, saying,
'Every household must take a lamb,
and on the fourteenth day, the community together
must slaughter the lambs at twilight.
Then you shall take the blood of the lambs
and put it upon the lintels of your houses and upon the doorposts.
And you shall roast the meat in a fire
and eat it on this night with flatbread and bitter herbs.

You shall eat it in haste
with sandals on your feet and your staffs in your hands,
for it is a Passover offering to Me.
And I will go through the land of Egypt,
and on this night I will strike down every firstborn in Egypt
and I will punish all the gods of Egypt.
I am Yahweh.
And the blood on your houses will be a sign—
I will see it and pass over you and you will not be destroyed.' "
The people gave homage and bowed low,
and what Yahweh had commanded Moses and Aaron,
this they did.

YAHWEH'S ARMY

And now at midnight
Yahweh struck down every firstborn
in the land of Egypt,
from the firstborn of
Pharaoh on his throne
to the firstborn of
the captive in the dungeon
to every firstborn of the beasts.

Pharaoh arose at night,
he and his servants and all Egypt,
and there was a great cry in the land,
for in every house someone was dead.

He called Moses and Aaron to him and said,
"Go out from here, you and the Israelites with you!
Go, worship God as you said!
Take your sheep and cattle—go, and plead for me."
And Egypt urged the people to leave, saying,
"Or we shall all be dead."

The Israelites took their dough in kneading bowls
wrapped in their clothing.
And they took the ornaments of silver and gold
they had asked of their neighbors, as Moses had said.
Thus they stripped the Egyptians.
They journeyed from Rameses to Succoth,
six hundred thousand men on foot,
and the women and children.
And they baked the dough they had brought into flatbread,
for it had not risen.
The people had been driven out of Egypt and could not delay.

The years the Israelites had dwelled in Egypt
were four hundred and thirty.
And at the end of that time,
on that very day,
Yahweh's army went out from the land of Egypt.

PILLAR OF FIRE

Moses spoke to the people, saying,
"Remember this day when you went out of Egypt
from the slave house.

And when Yahweh brings you to the land of the Canaanite
that He swore to your fathers about,
you must perform this festival in the month of the New Grain.
Seven days shall you eat flatbread,
and when your son asks, 'What does this mean?'
say to him, 'With a mighty hand, Yahweh brought us out of Egypt.'
And you shall keep this festival from year to year
and in every generation."

Now, when Pharaoh set the people free,
God led them not by the near road.
Instead He turned them around through the wilderness
at the Sea of Reeds.
The Israelites went up armed from the land of Egypt.
And Moses took Joseph's bones,
for Joseph had made the sons of Israel swear it, saying,
"God will reward you if you take my bones from here."
They set out from Succoth and camped at Etham,
at the edge of the wilderness.
Yahweh went before them in a pillar of cloud,
to lead them on the way,
and in a pillar of fire at night,
so that they could travel by day and night.

THE WATERS SPLIT APART

Pharaoh was told that the people had fled, and his heart changed.
He said, "Why did we let them go?"
Then he harnessed his chariot and he took six hundred warriors,
and their chariots and their captains.

Yahweh hardened the heart of Pharaoh, king of Egypt,
and he pursued the Israelites camped by the sea.

The Israelites lifted up their eyes,
and here, Egypt was coming toward them!
They were very afraid and they cried out to Yahweh.
And they said to Moses,
"Was it because there were no graves in Egypt
that you took us to die in the wilderness?
What have you done to us, bringing us out of Egypt?"
Moses said to the people, "Don't be afraid!
Be strong and Yahweh will deliver you.
The Egyptians that you see today you will never see again."

And Yahweh said to Moses,
"Let the Israelites go forward.
And you — you must raise your staff, stretch it above the sea,
and split it apart
so that the Israelites can come through the sea on dry ground.
But I will harden the heart of Egypt so that they come after you,
and I will be glorified through Pharaoh and his army."

The messenger of God who was going before the Israelites
moved back and went behind them.
And the pillar of cloud went behind them.
Now there was darkness and cloud — they lit up the night.
And Moses stretched out his hand over the sea.
And Yahweh drove it back with a roaring east wind.
The waters split apart and He made a path.
The Israelites came into the sea on dry ground,
the waters a wall for them on their right and on their left.

Pharaoh came after them,

with all his chariots and warriors and horses.

At daybreak Yahweh panicked the army of Egypt.

He locked the wheels of their chariots and drove them hard.

Egypt said, "Let me flee, for Yahweh is fighting for them!"

Then Yahweh said to Moses,

"Stretch your hand over the sea."

And Moses stretched his hand over the sea,

and the waters joined again

with Egypt's horses and army fleeing toward them.

And Yahweh hurled the Egyptians into the sea.

Not one of them remained.

But the Israelites went through the sea on dry ground,

and they saw the hand that Yahweh had raised against Egypt.

And the people feared Yahweh and they trusted in Him,

and in Moses, His servant.

WITH TIMBRELS AND DANCING

Then Moses and the Israelites sang a song to Yahweh, saying:

> "I will sing to Yahweh,
>
> for He has triumphed, yes, triumphed.
>
> The horse and its rider He flung into the sea!
>
> The waters covered them over.
>
> Down deep they went like a stone.
>
> Your right hand, Yahweh,
>
> shattered the enemy.
>
> With the breath of Your nostrils,

waters piled up.
The gushing streams stood like walls.

Who is like You among the gods, O Yahweh!
Who is like You, mighty in holiness,
awesome in splendor, worker of wonders!

The Canaanites hear; they shudder in fear.
Terror seizes them and they melt away.
Until Your people cross over, O Yahweh!
And You plant them in Your holy place."

Then Miriam the prophetess, Aaron's sister,
took a timbrel in her hand,
and all the women went out after her, with timbrels and dancing.
And Miriam sang to them:
"I will sing to Yahweh,
for He has triumphed, yes, triumphed.
The horse and its rider
He flung into the sea!"

In the Wilderness

THE WATER TURNED SWEET

And the Israelites traveled on from the Sea of Reeds.
They went three days into the wilderness and did not find water.
They came to the pool of Marah, but could not drink
because the water was bitter.
And the people murmured against Moses, saying,
"What shall we drink?"
Moses cried out to Yahweh, and Yahweh showed him a tree
and Moses threw it into the water, and the water turned sweet.

There Yahweh tested the Israelites, to see if they trusted in Him.
He said, "If you listen to My voice and do what is right in My eyes,
all that you need will be given.
And the plagues I put upon Egypt I will not put upon you,
for I am Yahweh, your healer."

And the people came to Elim.
There were twelve springs of water and seventy palm trees,
and they camped beside the water.

BREAD FROM THE HEAVENS

The Israelites traveled on
until they came into a wilderness between Elim and Sinai.
It was the fifteenth day of the second month
after their going out from the land of Egypt,
and there was no bread left.
Again the people murmured against Moses and Aaron, saying,
"You have brought us here to make us die by starvation.
If only we had died by Yahweh's hand in Egypt,
when we sat by the cauldrons of meat cooking
and ate our fill of bread!"

And Yahweh said to Moses,
"I will rain down bread from the heavens for you."
Then Moses and Aaron spoke to the Israelites and said,
"Yahweh will give you meat in the evening to eat,
and bread in the morning.
And you will see Yahweh's glory.

Do not test Him!
Not against us are your murmurings, but against Yahweh."
Then all the Israelites turned toward the wilderness
and Yahweh's glory appeared in the cloud.

In the evening, a flock of quail dropped upon the camp.
In the morning, dew was everywhere,
and as the sun rose and the dew lifted,
there was something white, like frost upon the ground.
When the people saw it, they said, "*Man hu:* What is it?"
And Moses said, "It is the bread that Yahweh has given you."

Now the house of Israel called it manna —
its taste is like a wafer in honey.

MASSAH AND MERIBAH

And the Israelites traveled on as Yahweh led them,
and they camped at Rephidim,
and there was no water for the people to drink.
For the third time, they murmured against Moses, saying,
"Why did you bring us up from Egypt
to make us die by thirst?"
And Moses cried out to Yahweh, saying:
            "What shall I do with this people?
            A little more and they will stone me!"
Yahweh said to Moses, "Go before the people,
and the staff with which you struck the Nile, take it in your hand.
Here, I will stand on the rock at Horeb,
and you will strike the rock and water will come from it,
and the people will drink."
And Moses did thus, before their eyes.
And he called the name of the place
Massah and *Meribah:* testing and quarreling,
because still the Israelites quarreled
and because still they tested Yahweh, saying,
"Is He among us or not?"

Now men from Amalek came and made war upon Israel.
And Moses said to Joshua, son of Nun, an attendant to him from youth,
"Choose men for us and go out against Amalek tomorrow.
I will stand on the hilltop, with the staff of God in my hand."
Aaron and Hur went with Moses.

When Moses raised his hand, Israel was winning.

And when he lowered it, Amalek was.

Moses's hands grew heavy,

and Aaron and Hur supported them, one on each side.

Then his hands were steady until the sun set,

and Joshua cut down Amalek with the edge of his sword.

A JUDGE UPON THE PEOPLE

Jethro, priest of Midian, Moses's father-in-law,

heard all that God had done for Moses and His people,

how Yahweh had brought the Israelites out of Egypt.

So Jethro took Moses's wife, Zipporah,

back to him in the wilderness

after she had been sent home with her two sons,

Gershom and Eliezer.

Moses went out to meet his father-in-law,

and they bowed low and kissed each other

and went into the tent.

Jethro said, "Blessed be Yahweh,

who delivered you from Egypt and set His people free.

Now I know that He is greater than all gods."

The next day, Moses sat as a judge upon the people,

and they stood before him from morning until evening.

And Jethro saw all Moses had to do for the Israelites,

and he said, "Why do you alone judge them?"

Moses said, "They come to me to make known

the laws and teachings of God

and so I can decide between one man and another."

Then Jethro said, "No, it is too hard.
You cannot do it alone.
And you will wear yourself out—and your people, too.
So now, listen to me:
You must select men you can trust, men who fear God,
and let them judge the people at all times.
In small matters, they shall judge for themselves,
but they shall bring large matters to you.
In this way you will share the burden,
and the people will come to the land in peace."

Moses did all that his father-in-law had said
and then sent him off to return to Midian.

At Sinai

ON THE WINGS OF EAGLES

On the third month after the Israelites went out from Egypt,

on that very day,

they came to the wilderness of Sinai

and they camped there before the mountain.

Now Moses went up to God,

and Yahweh called to him from the mountain, saying,

"Tell the Israelites, 'You have seen what I did to Egypt,

how I carried you on the wings of eagles

and brought you to Me.

So now, if you listen to My voice and keep My covenant,

you will be a treasure to Me among all peoples.
Truly, all the earth is Mine,
but you, you shall be to Me a kingdom of priests,
a holy nation.'"
Moses told these words to the Israelites,
and they answered together, saying,
"All that Yahweh has said, we will do."

Then Yahweh said to Moses,
"I am coming to you in a deep cloud
so that the people will hear Me speak to you,
and so they will trust in you for all time.
Now go to them—make them holy today and tomorrow,
let them scrub their clothes,
for on the third day, I will come down on Mount Sinai.
Set bounds for them, saying,
'Whoever touches the mountain, even the edge of the mountain—
he shall be put to death.'"

And it happened on the third day, when it was daybreak,
there was thunder and lightning,
and the sound of the ram's horn,
and a deep cloud was on the mountain.
All the people in the camp trembled.
And Moses led them out toward God.
Now Mount Sinai smoked
because Yahweh had come down upon it in a fire,
and the mountain shuddered,
and the sound of the ram's horn was deafening.
Then Yahweh called Moses to the mountaintop—
Moses, and Aaron with him.
And they went up.

THE WORDS OF GOD

God spoke all these words, saying,
"I am Yahweh, your God,
who brought you out of the land of Egypt,
from the house of slaves.

"You shall have no other gods before Me.
You shall make no carved image
of what is in the heavens above
or the earth below
or the waters beneath.
You shall not bow down to them or serve them,
for I, Yahweh, I am a jealous God.
You shall not take the name of Yahweh your God in vain.

"Remember the Sabbath day, to keep it holy.
On six days you shall work,
but the seventh day is a Sabbath for Me.
For in six days Yahweh made the heavens and earth
and the sea and all that is in it,
and on the seventh day He rested.

"Honor your father and your mother
that you may long endure on the earth.
Do not murder.
Do not commit adultery.
Do not steal.

"Do not speak falsely against your neighbor.
Do not covet your neighbor's house
or your neighbor's wife

or his slave

or his ox or his ass."

And all the people saw the thunder and the light flashing

and the sound of the ram's horn and the mountain smoking.

They saw, and they stood at a distance.

The Israelites said to Moses, "Speak to us and we will obey,

but do not let God speak to us again or we will die."

Then Moses approached the thick cloud where God was

and God gave Moses laws to set before the people.

And Moses wrote down the words of God and His laws—

they were a Book of the Covenant.

Early in the morning, Moses set up an altar at the foot of the mountain,

with twelve pillars for the twelve tribes of Israel.

And the Israelites burned offerings and sacrificed bulls to Yahweh,

and Moses threw the blood on the people, saying,

"Now the covenant is sealed."

Then Moses and Aaron,

and Aaron's first two sons Nadab and Abihu,

and seventy of the elders of Israel

went up and bowed to Yahweh from far away.

Beneath His feet was a purity like sapphire tiles.

They saw the God of Israel,

and they ate and drank.

And God spoke to Moses, saying,

"Go up to Me on the mountain

and I will give you stone tablets

with My commandments to teach them."

Moses went up;

he was on the mountain for forty days and forty nights.

And God said,
"Let the Israelites make Me a Tabernacle
so that I might dwell among them.
There I will speak with you and the Israelites,
and I will sanctify Aaron and his sons to be My priests.
And My presence shall be in your midst,
and I will be your God.
According to all I say to you,
in its form and design, thus shall you make the Tabernacle."

When God finished speaking with Moses on Mount Sinai,
He gave him the two tablets of the covenant,
stone tablets written by the finger of God.

A GOLDEN CALF

The people saw that Moses was long
in coming down from the mountain,
and they assembled against Aaron and said to him,
"Come, make us a god who can go before us,
for this man Moses, who brought us from Egypt—
we do not know what has happened to him."

Aaron said to them,
"Take the gold rings that are on the ears of your wives,
your sons and daughters, and bring them to me."
Aaron took the gold rings and cast them in a mold
and made them into a golden calf.
Then the people said, "Here is your god, O Israel,
who brought you from the land of Egypt."

And Aaron built an altar to it and said,
"Tomorrow is a festival to Yahweh."
The Israelites rose early the next day
and brought burnt offerings
and they sat down to eat and drink,
and they danced and played.

Yahweh said to Moses,
"Hurry. Go down,
for your people that I brought from Egypt—
they are bringing ruin on themselves."

And Yahweh said, "They are a stiff-necked people,
and My anger will blaze against them.
But of you I will make a great nation."
Moses pleaded with his God, saying,
"Do you want the Egyptians to say,
'With an evil plan He brought the Israelites out
to kill them in the mountains?'
Turn back Your anger and relent!
Remember Abraham and Isaac and Jacob,
Your servants to whom You said,
'I will make your children like the stars of the heavens
and the land I promised you, I will give to your children
so that they may have it forever.'"
And Yahweh relented from the evil He planned against His people.

Now Moses turned and came down the mountain,
with the two tablets of the covenant in his hand,
and the writing on them was God's writing.
And when Moses came near the camp

and he saw the calf and the dancing,
his anger blazed and he threw the tablets away
and smashed them at the bottom of the mountain.
He took the calf and burned it in a fire
and ground it into fine powder and threw it on the water
and made the Israelites drink.

Aaron said to Moses, "Do not let your anger blaze!
You yourself know this people — how they are set on evil."
Then Moses saw that the people were out of control,
for Aaron had let them lose control.

And Moses stood near the camp and said,
"Whoever is for Yahweh, come to me!"
And the tribe of Levi gathered around him.
Moses said to them, "Thus says Yahweh, the God of Israel,
'Each man put his sword on his thigh and go from gate to gate,
and each man kill his brother and his neighbor and his kin,
whoever led this rebellion.'"

The Levites did as Moses said,
and three thousand men died on that day.
Then Moses said to the Israelites,
"You have committed a great crime.
Now I will go up to Yahweh. Perhaps I can atone for it."
And Moses went back to Yahweh and said,
"Forgive them. Or take my life in place of theirs."
Yahweh said,
"The one who has offended Me, he alone will die."

IN THE CLEFT OF THE ROCK

Then Yahweh said,
"Now lead this people to the land
that I swore to Abraham, Isaac, and Jacob, saying,
'To your children will I give it.'
But I will not go in your midst, for you are a stiff-necked people,
and I would destroy you on the way."
When the people heard this, they mourned,
stripping off their ornaments.

And now Moses would take the tent
and pitch it for himself far from the camp,
and he called it the Tent of Meeting.
And the pillar of cloud would come to the Tent
and Yahweh would speak with Moses face-to-face,
as a man speaks to a friend.

Moses said to Him, "This nation is Your people.
If Your presence does not come in our midst,
do not take us up from here.
Pray, if I have found favor in Your eyes,
stay with us so that I and Your people are set apart
from every other people on the face of the earth."
And Yahweh said to Moses,
"What you have asked Me, I will do,
for truly you have gained My favor
and I have known you by name."
Then Moses said, "Then let me know Your ways.
Let me see Your glory!"

And Yahweh said, "You will not see My face,
for no human can see Me and live."
And He said, "Stand on the rock
and when My glory passes you,
I will put you in the cleft of the rock
and shield you with the palm of My hand
until I pass by.
Then I will put down My hand
and you will see My back.
But My face will not be seen."

TWO STONE TABLETS

Yahweh said to Moses,
"Carve two stone tablets like the first,
and I will write on them
the words that were on the ones you smashed.
In the morning you must go up the mountain alone."

Moses went up on Mount Sinai,
and he took the two stone tablets in his hand.
And Yahweh came to him in the cloud,
calling out: "Yahweh, Yahweh!
A God compassionate and gracious,
slow to anger,
kind and faithful,
extending kindness to the thousandth generation,
forgiving offense and crime,
yet carrying the crimes of fathers to the sons and the sons' sons
in the third and fourth generations."

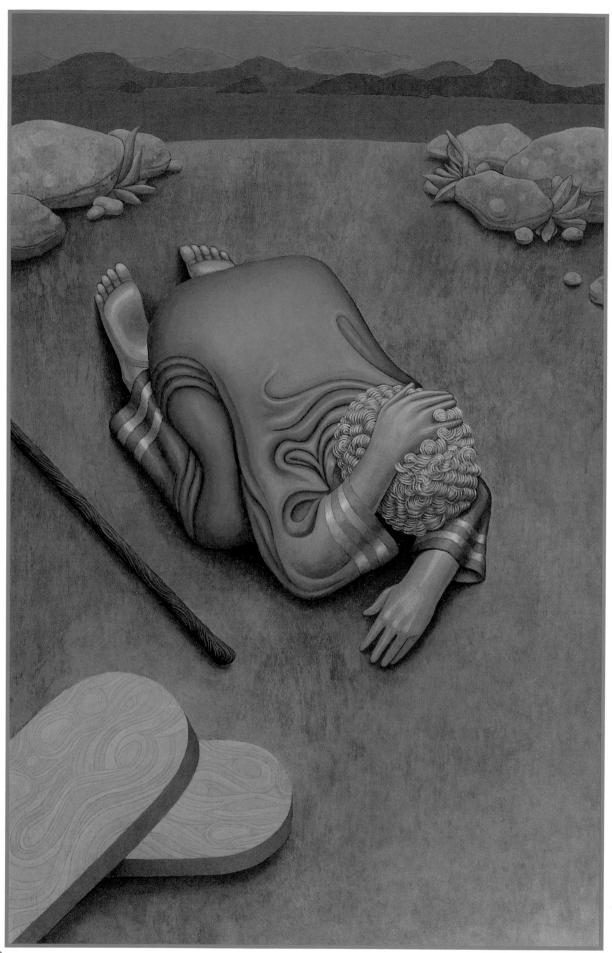

At once Moses fell to the ground and bowed low, saying,

"Pray forgive our crime and claim us as Yours."

Then Yahweh gave Moses the words of the covenant with Israel,

the Ten Words,

and Moses wrote them on the tablets.

And again he was there with Yahweh forty days and forty nights.

He ate no bread and drank no water.

And when he came down from the mountain

with the two tablets in his hand,

Moses did not know that the skin of his face radiated light

because he had spoken with God.

Aaron and all the Israelites saw Moses,

and look, he radiated light!

So they were afraid to come near.

Moses called to them, and they approached,

and then he commanded them

all that Yahweh had said on Mount Sinai.

INDIGO AND VIOLET AND CRIMSON

Now Moses assembled the community of Israelites

and said to them as before,

"For six days you shall work, but on the seventh you shall rest,

for it is a Sabbath for Yahweh.

"This is what Yahweh has commanded:

Let everyone whose heart is moved bring gifts for Him.

And let skilled men come, to make the Tabernacle

for His dwelling, its coverings and furnishings,

and the sacred garments for Aaron, the priest, and his sons.

And they shall make an ark of acacia wood
overlaid with pure gold inside and out.
And in the ark you shall set
the tablets of the covenant."

Then everyone, men and women, too, brought gifts—
indigo and violet and crimson yarns,
fine linen and ram skins and embroidered work,
gold earrings and bracelets, and the women's bronze mirrors.
Then the people were held back from bringing,
and skilled men performed the tasks Yahweh had commanded,
to His form and design.
And when the work was completed,
they brought the Tabernacle to Moses
and he saw it and he blessed them all.

YAHWEH'S GLORY FILLED THE TABERNACLE

On the first day of the first month in the second year,
Moses set up the Tabernacle as Yahweh had commanded.
He spread the tent over it from above,
as Yahweh had commanded.
He took the Covenant and set it inside the Ark,
as Yahweh had commanded.
He lit the lamp and placed the altars,
as Yahweh had commanded.
He offered up a burnt offering and a grain offering,
as Yahweh had commanded.
And so Moses finished the work.

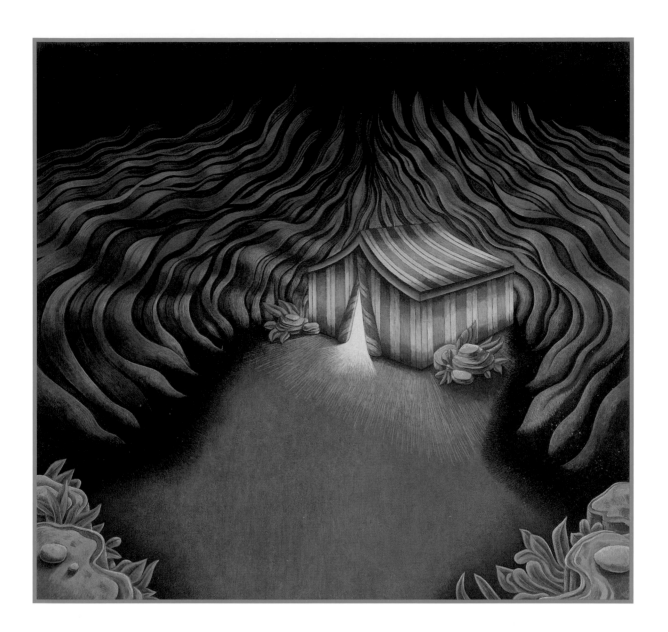

Now the cloud covered the Tent of Meeting,
and Yahweh's glory filled the Tabernacle.
When the cloud lifted, they would set out on their journeys,
but when it did not lift, they would remain.
And the cloud of Yahweh dwelled in the Tabernacle by day,
and fire was in it by night,
before the eyes of the House of Israel.

LEVITICUS

ויקרא

SMOKE ON THE ALTAR

Now Yahweh called to Moses from the Tent of Meeting
and He said, "Command the Israelites, saying,
'Anyone who brings an offering to Me from the herd or the flock
must put his hand on the animal and slay it before Me.
And the priest shall burn the animal and turn it to smoke on the altar.
It is a burnt offering, a fire offering to Yahweh.

'And anyone who brings a grain offering to Me
must bring the best flour and pour oil on it and put incense on it.
And the priest shall turn it to smoke on the altar.
It is a fire offering to Yahweh.'"

And Yahweh said to Moses,
"Command Aaron and his sons, saying,
'The flame on the altar must not go out;
it is a perpetual fire.
And the priest shall eat a portion of the offerings in a holy place;
it is the holy of holies.'"

OIL AND BLOOD

The community assembled at the Tent of Meeting,
and Moses brought Aaron and his sons forward
and washed them with water and put the sacred garments on them,
as Yahweh had commanded.
Then he anointed the Tabernacle with oil
and poured blood on the altar.
And he anointed Aaron and his sons with oil and blood
and consecrated them, saying,
"You shall sit at the Tent of Meeting for seven days
as Yahweh has charged so that you will not die."

Now on the eighth day,
Moses called Aaron and his sons, and the elders of Israel,
and told them to speak to the Israelites, saying,
"Bring forward animal offerings and grain offerings,
then the glory of Yahweh will appear to you."
The people brought them, and Aaron and his sons

turned the offerings to smoke on the altar.
And Moses and Aaron went into the Tent of Meeting,
then they came out and blessed the Israelites.
And the glory of God came from Yahweh as a fire
and consumed the burnt offering.
And the people saw, and shouted, and fell upon their faces.

WITH ALIEN FIRE

And now Aaron's sons Nadab and Abihu each took a fire pan
and put incense in it, and offered it to Yahweh with alien fire,
which He had not commanded.
Then fire came from Yahweh
and consumed them
so that they died in His presence.
And Moses said to Aaron,
"It must be only as He commanded."
Aaron was silent. His sons were dead.

Then Moses called to Nadab and
Abihu's cousins
to take their bodies from the
sacred place
and carry them outside the camp.
Now Moses said to Aaron,
and to Eleazar and Ithamar,
Aaron's two sons who remained,
"You shall not tear your hair or rip
your garments in mourning.
The community may weep for the burning,
but you must stay at the Tent of Meeting

for the oil of His anointing is upon you.
And so there is separation
between the holy and the profane,
and between the clean and unclean.
And you must teach the Israelites His laws.
Take a portion of the grain offering and the fire offering
and eat it at the altar, for it is holy of holies."

And Aaron said to Moses,
"How could I eat it when such things have happened to me?
If I were to eat, would it seem good in the eyes of Yahweh?"
And Moses heard.

A DAY OF ATONEMENT

Yahweh spoke to Moses after the death of Aaron's two sons,
who died when they came forward before Him.
And He said, "Speak to Aaron so that he will come
into the sacred place, the holy of holies,
and will not die.
He must bathe himself in water,
and dress in a linen tunic and turban.
And from the Israelites he shall take two goats and a ram for offerings,
and a bull of offering from his own household.
Two lots shall be placed upon the goats—
one is marked for Yahweh, and the other is to be sent away.

"Then Aaron shall go into the sanctuary.
He shall go behind the curtain to the holy of holies
and put incense upon the fire so that the cloud from the incense
screens the presence of Yahweh.

Then he is to purify the sanctuary with the blood of the offerings
and atone for himself and for all the community.
Then Aaron shall bring forward the live goat
and confess the sins of the Israelites with his two hands upon it.
And he shall place the sins of the Israelites upon its head.
Next, a man who has been chosen shall take the goat
and send it into the wilderness, with the sins of the Israelites upon it.
And the goat shall be set free.

"And this shall be a law upon you for all time:
In the seventh month, on the tenth day of the month,
you shall afflict yourselves; no work shall you do.
It is a Sabbath of Sabbaths for you, a day of atonement for you.
And you shall be made pure."

A COVENANT FOREVER

And Yahweh spoke to Moses, saying,
"Speak to the Israelites and say to them,
'I am Yahweh, your God.
Do not follow the ways of the land of Egypt, where you dwelled,
or of the land of Canaan, where I am taking you.
My ways alone you must follow. My laws you must observe.
You shall be holy, for I, Yahweh, am holy.

'When you harvest your field,
do not harvest to the edges of the field or gather the gleanings;
do not pick your vineyard bare.
But leave the fruit for the poor and the sojourner.
I am Yahweh.

'Do not lie or cheat your fellow man or do injustice.

Do not hate your family in your heart.

Do not take vengeance.

Love your fellow man as yourself.

My Sabbath you shall keep, My sanctuary revere.

Do not mistreat the sojourner among you,

for you were all sojourners in the land of Egypt.

I am Yahweh.'"

And Yahweh spoke to Moses, saying,

"Command the Israelites to take the clear oil of beaten olives

for kindling the lamp in the Tent of Meeting.

It shall burn from evening until morning, perpetually before Yahweh.

It is a law for all time.

And on Sabbath days the Israelites shall bake twelve loaves

and place them before Yahweh on the golden table.

It is a covenant forever."

AN EYE FOR AN EYE

A man came among the Israelites;

he was the son of an Israelite woman and an Egyptian man.

And a fight broke out in the camp,

and the son of the Israelite woman cursed Yahweh's name.

Then he was brought to Moses and placed under guard.

And Yahweh said to Moses,

"Take the blasphemer out beyond the camp,

and let those who heard his curse lay their hands on his head,

and the community shall stone him.

For blaspheming Yahweh's name, he shall be put to death."

And Yahweh said to Moses,
"Speak to the Israelites, saying,
'And if a man kills another human being, he shall be put to death.
As he has done, so shall it be done to him—
an eye for an eye, a tooth for a tooth.'"
Thus said Moses to the people.
Then they took the blasphemer out beyond the camp
and pelted him with stones until he was dead.

MY DWELLING WILL BE IN YOUR MIDST

And Yahweh spoke to Moses on Mount Sinai:
"Say to the Israelites, 'I am Yahweh.
If you observe My laws and keep My commands,
I will favor you with rains in their season.
The earth will yield its harvest and the vines their fruit.
There will be peace in the land
and no wild beast will threaten you.
You will pursue your enemies and they will fall before your sword.
I will fulfill My covenant with you.
My dwelling will be in your midst.
I am Yahweh, who brought you out of Egypt
and broke the bars of your yoke
and let you walk upright.

'But if you do not obey Me and keep My commandments
I will bring upon you shock and sickness.
Your enemies will vanquish you and you will flee.
And if you still do not obey Me,
I will make your heavens like iron and your earth like bronze
and send wild beasts to carry off your children.

And if you still do not obey Me,

I will make your land desolate and your cities a ruin

and scatter you among the nations.

And you will have fear in your hearts.

The sound of a driven leaf will make you flee

and you will fall, though there is no pursuer.

Each man will stumble against his brother, as upon a sword.

You shall perish among the nations,

and the land of your enemies shall consume you.

And those who are left will confess their guilt

and the guilt of their fathers

in abandoning Me and breaking My commands.

Their stubborn hearts will become humble

and they will atone.

'Then I will remember My covenant with Jacob

and My covenant with Isaac

and My covenant with Abraham.

I will remember the land.

And I will not destroy My people or end My covenant with them,

for I am Yahweh.' "

NUMBERS

במדבר

BY THEIR FATHERS' HOUSES

Yahweh spoke to Moses in the wilderness of Sinai

in the Tent of Meeting.

It was the first day of the second month,

in the second year of their going out from Egypt.

And He said,

"You must count the community of the Israelites.

Count them by their fathers' houses,

all men twenty and older who are able to go into battle.

And let there be a man from each tribe, a chieftain to stand with you."

Now, all the men who were counted from their fathers' houses
were six hundred three thousand five hundred and fifty.
But Aaron and the Levites were not counted among them,
for Yahweh spoke to Moses, saying,
"The tribe of Levi you are not to count.
They are to care for the Tabernacle,
to surround it in the camp and carry it on our journeys."

Yahweh said,
"And thus shall Aaron bless the Israelites before starting out.
Say to them:

> 'May Yahweh bless you and protect you.
> May He shine His face upon you and favor you.
> May He lift up His face to you and give you peace.'"

And Yahweh said to Moses,
"Make two trumpets of hammered silver.
They shall be for you to summon the community
and set the tribes in motion.
The sound of the trumpets shall be a reminder for the ages —
I am Yahweh."

And now each tribe was assembled under its banner
in the order of the march.
And on the twentieth day of the month,
the cloud lifted from the Tabernacle of the Covenant
and the Israelites began their journeys.
They left the wilderness of Sinai,
and when the cloud came to rest again, they camped.
It was in the wilderness of Paran.
And so they were led from the beginning by the word of God.

They marched for three days
and the Ark of the Covenant went before them.
When the cloud lifted, Moses would say,
        "Arise, O Yahweh, and scatter Your enemies.
           Your foes will flee before You."
And when it came to rest, he would say,
        "Return, O Yahweh, to Israel's multitudes."

QUAILS FROM THE SEA

The people began complaining with evil words before Yahweh,
and Yahweh heard.
His anger flamed wildly. His fire licked at the edges of the camp.
The people cried out to Moses,
and he asked Yahweh to stop the fire
and it died down.
And they called that place *Taberah:* blaze.

Then the people craved meat.
They wept and said, "Who will give us meat to eat?
We remember the fish in Egypt,
the cucumber, the melons, the leeks, the onions, the garlic.
But now our throats are parched.
There is nothing here, nothing! Only manna before our eyes."

Moses heard the people weeping,
and Yahweh's anger flamed again, and in Moses's eyes, that was evil.
Moses said to Yahweh,
"Why have You dealt so harshly with me
and put the burden of this people upon me?

Did I conceive this people, did I give birth to them,
that You should say to me,
'Carry them in your lap, as a parent carries an infant.
Take them to the land that I promised to their fathers?
Where am I to get meat to give this people
when they weep to me, asking for meat?
I cannot carry this people alone. They are too heavy for me.
If I have found favor in your eyes,
kill me, yes, kill me now."

Then Yahweh said to Moses,
"Gather seventy elders at the Tent of Meeting,
and I shall come down.
Place My spirit that is upon you also upon them,
and they will bear the burden of the people with you
so that you do not have to bear it alone.

"And you must say to the Israelites,
'Tomorrow you will eat meat, for you wept to Yahweh, saying,
"Give us meat. It was better for us in Egypt."
You will have meat!
Not for one day or two, not for five days or ten or twenty.
No, you will eat meat for a month of days
until it comes out of your nostrils
and becomes loathsome to you.
For you have scorned Yahweh, who is in your midst,
by weeping and longing for Egypt.'"

Then a wind moved fast from Yahweh
and swept in quails from the sea
and spread them all around the camp.
They were piled on the ground, high as a man's knee.

The people arose that day and began gathering the quail.
The meat was still caught between their teeth, not chewed,
when Yahweh's anger blazed among the people
and He felled them with a terrible plague.
That place was called *Kivrot Ha-Taava:* the Graves of Craving.
Then the Israelites left and journeyed to Hazeroth.

O GOD, PLEASE HEAL HER!

And Miriam, with Aaron, spoke against Moses
because of the Cushite wife he had taken.
They said, "Is it only through Moses that Yahweh has spoken?
Has He not spoken through us, too?"
And Yahweh heard.

Now, Moses was a humble man,
more than any other on earth.
And Yahweh said suddenly,
"Go out, the three of you, to the Tent of Meeting."
He stood at the entrance in a pillar of cloud
and called to Aaron and Miriam.
He said, "Listen to Me.
If a prophet came among you,
I would show Myself to him in a vision
or speak to him in a dream.
Not so Moses.
I speak to him face-to-face, not in riddles.
And the face of Yahweh he beholds.
So why were you not afraid to speak against him?"

Then Yahweh's anger rose up,
and when the cloud moved away from the Tent,
look, Miriam's skin was bleached with snow-white scales.

Aaron said to Moses, "I beg you,

do not make her suffer for our guilt."

And Moses cried out to Yahweh, "O God, please heal her! Please."

And Yahweh said,

"She must be kept outside the camp for seven days

to bear her shame."

The people did not leave Hazeroth

until Miriam was taken back in.

Then they camped in the wilderness of Paran.

SCOUTING THE LAND

Yahweh spoke to Moses, saying,

"Send men to scout the land of Canaan

that I am giving to the Israelites.

One man each for his father's tribe, each one a leader."

And Moses sent them, twelve men,

and among them were Caleb, son of Japhunneh,

and Joshua, son of Nun.

And he said to them,

"Go up through the Negev and then into the hill country.

See what kind of land it is. Is it good or bad?

Are the people few or many?

Are there trees? Is the soil rich?

And you must bring back the fruit of the land."

It was the season of the first ripe grapes.

So the men went up and scouted the land as far as Hebron.

They cut down a cluster of grapes so heavy

that two men had to carry it on a pole.
And they saw the people, the Anakim.
After forty days, they returned from scouting the land.

The twelve men came before Moses and Aaron
and all the Israelites, and showed them the grapes, saying,
"Yes, the land where you sent us is flowing with milk and honey —
look, here is the fruit."
Caleb and Joshua said,
"Let us go up there. We can take the land."
But the other scouts said,
"The people of that land are fierce, and the towns are walled.
We cannot attack that people."
And they spread lies among the Israelites, saying,
"The country we scouted devours those who dwell there.
The people we saw are the descendants of a giant.
We were like grasshoppers to them!"

FORTY YEARS FOR FORTY DAYS

All in the community lifted their voices and wept through the night.
And they murmured against Moses and Aaron, saying,
"Is Yahweh taking us to that land to kill us by the sword?
If only we had not left Egypt!
If only we could die in this wilderness!"

Moses and Aaron fell on their faces.
And Caleb and Joshua ripped their garments in mourning.
And they said to the Israelites, "If Yahweh favors us,
He will bring us to that land and give it to us.

Do not be afraid of the people of the land.
If Yahweh is with us, they will be our prey.
Do not rebel against Him!"
But the Israelites moved to pelt them with stones.

Then the glory of Yahweh came before all the community
in the Tent of Meeting.
And Yahweh said to Moses,
"How long will this people scorn Me?
How long will they not trust in Me?
I will strike them down and disown them—each one but you."
And Moses said, "Pray, let Your power be as You have spoken:
'A God compassionate and gracious,
slow to anger,
kind and faithful,
extending kindness to the thousandth generation,
forgiving offense and crime,
yet carrying the crimes of fathers to the sons and the sons' sons
in the third and fourth generations.'
Forgive this people,
as You have forgiven them since Egypt!"

And Yahweh said,
"I forgive them as you ask.
But as I live and as My glory fills the world,
all the men who have tested Me ten times over
shall never see the land I promised to their fathers.
Say to them,
'Just as you have asked, Yahweh will do to you:
Your corpses shall fall in this wilderness,
and your children shall wander in the wilderness for forty years

until your corpses come to an end.
By the number of days that the land was scouted,
forty years for forty days,
you will bear your punishment.
Then you will know what it is to oppose Me!
Only Caleb and Joshua, who remained true,
shall live to enter the land.'"

The Israelites mourned greatly.
And they started early in the morning
to go up into the hill country, saying,
"We will go to the land that Yahweh has promised,
for we were wrong."
But Moses said, "Why are you again going against Him?
Do not go up, for Yahweh is not in your midst!"
But the people still went,
marching to the top of the mountains.
And the Amalekites and Canaanites, who dwelled there,
came and shattered them at Hormah.

THE UNDERWORLD

Korah from the tribe of Levi,
and Dathan and Abiram from the tribe of Reuben,
together with two hundred and fifty Israelites
rose up against Moses and Aaron,
saying, "Why should you rule us?
All the people are holy, all of them,
and Yahweh is in their midst."

When Moses heard, he fell on his face.
And he said to Korah and all who were with him,
"In the morning, Yahweh will show you
who is His and who is holy."

Then he said, "Each man must take his fire pan
and place incense upon it and bring it to Yahweh,
two hundred and fifty fire pans, along with Aaron's."
And each man did,
standing at the entrance to the Tent of Meeting,
and all the community assembled with them,
against Moses and Aaron.

Then the glory of Yahweh came into the Tent of Meeting
and He said to Moses and Aaron,
"Remove yourselves from this community
and I will put an end to them!"
Aaron and Moses fell on their faces, saying,
"When one man sins, shall You punish every man?"
Yahweh said to Moses, "Move the people
from the tents of Korah, Dathan, and Abiram,
for they rose up against you."

Now the three men came out and stood by their tents
with their wives and their sons and their little ones.
And Moses said, "If these men die as all men do,
and if their death is like other deaths,
you will know it was not Yahweh who sent me to lead you.
But if the ground opens its mouth and swallows them
and they go down alive into *Sheol:* the underworld,
then you will know these men have scorned Yahweh."

And it happened, as soon as Moses finished speaking,
that the ground split open beneath them,
and swallowed them up
with their households and all that was theirs.
They went down alive to Sheol and perished.

The Israelites who were around them fled at the sound,
saying, "The earth might swallow us, too!"
And now fire went out from Yahweh
and consumed the two hundred and fifty men who were
bringing the incense.

BETWEEN THE DEAD AND THE LIVING

The next day, the Israelites
murmured against Moses and Aaron, saying,
"It is you who have brought death to Yahweh's people."
Then the cloud covered the Tent of Meeting,
and Yahweh's glory appeared.
And Yahweh said to Moses,
"Move away so that I might destroy them in an instant."
Moses and Aaron fell upon their faces, and Moses said,
"Go, Aaron, and take your fire pan
and put in it fire from the altar and place incense upon it
and carry it quickly to the Israelites to atone for them.
For wrath has gone out from Yahweh.
The plague has begun!"

And Aaron took the fire pan
and ran into the midst of the people.
Now the plague had begun against them.
He stood between the dead and the living,

and the plague was held back.
And those who died in the plague
were fourteen thousand and seven hundred,
beside those who had died with Korah.

And the people said to Moses,
"When will we be done with perishing?
We are lost; all of us are lost!"

AND MOSES RAISED HIS HAND

The Israelites, at the end of that generation,
came to the wilderness of Zin,
in the first month of the fortieth year.
The people stayed in Kadesh,
and Miriam died and was buried there.

The community had no water,
and they quarreled with Moses, saying,
"If only we had died when our brothers died!
Why did you take us out of Egypt to this evil place,
without water to drink?"
Moses and Aaron came away from the Israelites
to the Tent of Meeting and fell upon their faces.
Then Yahweh's glory appeared to them.
And He spoke to Moses, saying,
"Take the staff and bring together the people —
you and Aaron, your brother —
and before their eyes speak to the rock
so that it will bring forth water.
And then give them water to drink and to their cattle, too."

So Moses and Aaron brought the people together
in front of the rock, and Moses said to them,
"Now, you rebels, hear me!
From this rock we will bring forth water!"
And Moses raised his hand and struck the rock
two times with his staff.
And water poured out, and the people and their cattle drank.

And Yahweh said to Moses and to Aaron,
"Because you did not speak to the rock to bring forth water
but struck it yourself,
because you did not trust Me,
because you did not sanctify Me before the Israelites,

you shall never lead this community
into the land I gave them."
These were the waters of Meribah,
where the Israelites quarreled with Yahweh.

AARON AND ELEAZAR

They were close to Canaan now,
and Moses sent messengers to the king of Edom.
"Thus says your brother Israel:
You know the hardships we endured in Egypt.
We cried out to Yahweh, and He heard our voice.
Now we are at the border of your territory;
pray let us pass through it.
We will not trample your field or vineyard.
We will not drink water from your well.
We will stay on the king's road,
turning neither to the right nor left."
And Edom said to him,
"You shall not pass through me,
or I will meet you with the sword!"

The Israelites said,
"We will keep to the beaten track,
and if we drink your water, we will pay for it.
Pray allow us to pass. It is a small matter."
But Edom said, "You shall not pass!"
and came out with many armed men to meet them.
Then Israel turned away from Edom.

They marched on and came to Mount Hor,
and Yahweh spoke to Moses and Aaron, saying,

"Let Aaron be gathered to his kinsmen,
for he shall not enter the land I gave the Israelites
since you both rebelled against My word
at the waters of Meribah.
Take Aaron and Eleazar, his son, up on the mountain.
And strip Aaron's garments from him
and clothe Eleazar in his garments."

And Aaron died on the mountain.
When Moses came down from the mountain
and Eleazar with him,
all the community saw.
And they mourned thirty days for Aaron.

ACROSS THE JORDAN RIVER

And the Israelites marched through the Negev.
The Canaanite king of Arad waged war against them,
but Yahweh gave the Israelites victory.
They marched from Mount Hor to the Sea of Reeds
around the land of Edom.
And they sent messengers to Sihon, king of the Amorites,
asking if they could pass through his country.
But Sihon would not let them pass,
and he went against Israel with armed men.
Then Israel put him to the sword
and took the towns of the Amorites.

The Israelites marched on
and they camped on the plains of Moab,
across the Jordan River from Jericho,
which was in Canaan.

THE SORCERER BALAAM

Moab was frightened because the Israelites were so many,
and Moab said, "This horde will lick clean
all that is around us as the ox licks the grass of the field."
Then Balak, who was king of Moab,
sent elders to the sorcerer Balaam, saying,
"There is a people who came out of Egypt—
it covers the earth and has settled near me.
Come, put a curse on this people so I can drive it away!
For I know that whomever you bless is blessed,
and whomever you damn is damned."

In the morning, Balaam arose and
saddled his she-ass
and went with the elders of Moab.

And Yahweh's anger flamed because he was going,
so Yahweh's messenger stood in the road.
The she-ass saw Yahweh's messenger, his sword in his hand,
so she swerved and went into the field.
Balaam struck the she-ass to turn her back on the road,
but Yahweh's messenger stood on a path in the vineyard.
And the she-ass saw Yahweh's messenger
and she pressed against the wall,
and once again Balaam struck her.
Then Yahweh's messenger crossed over, standing in a narrow place —
there was nowhere to turn.
And the she-ass saw the messenger, so she lay down under Balaam,
and Balaam beat her with a stick.

Then Yahweh opened the mouth of the she-ass,
and she said to Balaam, "Why did you strike me three times?"
And Balaam said, "You were mocking me.
I should have killed you!"
Then the she-ass said to him, "Am I not your she-ass
that you have always ridden until this day?
Have I ever done it before?"
He said, "No."

Then Yahweh uncovered Balaam's eyes,
and he saw Yahweh's messenger standing before him,
his sword in his hand.
Balaam bowed down to the ground.
And Yahweh's messenger said to him,
"If your she-ass had not swerved away from me,
I would have killed you by now."

HOW GOOD YOUR TENTS, O ISRAEL

At daybreak Balak took Balaam to the high place of Baal
so that he could see the edge of the people to curse them.
Then Balaam went off by himself.
And God met Balaam and told him what to say to Balak.
So Balaam said:

> "Balak led me to curse Jacob,
>
> to speak of Israel's doom.
>
> How can I curse whom God has not cursed?
>
> May I die the death of the upright.
>
> May my fate be like theirs!"

Then Balak took Balaam to the top of Mount Pisgah
to curse the Israelites.
And Yahweh again put words in Balaam's mouth:

> "When He blesses, I cannot change it.
>
> He sees no evil in Jacob,
>
> no trouble in Israel.
>
> Yahweh, their god, is with them.
>
> Look, a people who rises like a lion,
>
> leaps up like the king of beasts!"

Then Balak took Balaam to the top of Peor.
Balaam turned his face to the wilderness,
and he saw for the first time all of Israel before him.
And the spirit of God came upon Balaam, and Balaam said:

> "Utters Balaam, with open eyes,
>
> 'How good your tents, O Israel,
>
> like gardens beside a river,
>
> like trees planted by Yahweh!
>
> Their kingdoms shall be exalted.

Blessed are they who blessed you,
cursed are they who curse you.'"

Balak struck his hands together and said to Balaam,
"I called you to curse my enemies,
and instead you have blessed them three times!"
Then Balaam said,
"Here is what this people will do to you in days to come:

A star goes forth from Jacob.
A meteor arises from Israel.
It smashes the forehead of Moab,
and Edom will be taken."

Then Balaam returned to his place, and Balak, too, went on his way.

THE ACCOUNTING

Israel stayed camped there on the plains,
and Yahweh said to Moses and to Eleazar, son of Aaron, the priest,
"Count the community of the Israelites,
all men twenty years and older, by their tribes and by their clans.
Count everyone going in the army."
And on the plains of Moab overlooking Jericho,
Moses and Eleazar counted the men
as Yahweh had commanded.
Many had died who rebelled against Moses and Aaron,
when they rebelled against Yahweh —
among them were Dathan and Abiram and Korah,
and the two hundred and fifty men consumed by fire.

And the number of the Israelites
was counted at six hundred and one thousand seven hundred
and thirty.

Then Yahweh said to Moses,
"Among these the land shall be divided in shares,
with the larger tribes and clans receiving more,
and the smaller tribes and clans less."
The Levites were not counted with the Israelites
because they were not given land.
But the men among the Levites were twenty-three thousand.
And Nadab and Abihu had died
when they brought alien fire before Yahweh.

Thus was the accounting of the Israelites
by Moses and Eleazar on the plains of Moab,
across the Jordan River from Jericho.
Not one of the men counted
were among those counted by Moses and Aaron
in the wilderness of Sinai.
For Yahweh had said of them,
"They are doomed to die in the wilderness."
And of that generation only Caleb and Joshua
were left.

The daughters of Zelophehad, of the tribe of Joseph,
came forward.
Their names were Mahlah, Noah, Hoglah, Milcah, and Tirzah.
And they said to Moses and Eleazar,
"Our father died in the wilderness and he had no sons.
Should we not have land among his clan
so that his name will not be lost?"
Then Yahweh spoke to Moses, saying,

"The daughters of Zelophehad speak rightfully.
You must pass on their father's portion to them,
and this shall be a law for the Israelites for all time."

IT SHALL COME TO PASS

Yahweh spoke to Moses, saying,
"Go up to the heights of Abiram
and see the land that I am giving to the Israelites.
And when you have seen it,
you will be gathered to your kinsmen—
you, even you, as Aaron, your brother, was gathered.
For you rebelled against Me in the wilderness of Zin
and did not sanctify Me before the Israelites
at the waters of Meribah."

Then Moses said,
"Let Yahweh, God of the spirits of all the living,
appoint a man over the community
who will go before them in battle
and who will lead them out and take them back,
so that Yahweh's people will not be like sheep
who have no shepherd."
And Yahweh said to Moses,
"Take Joshua, son of Nun, a man of spirit,
and lay your hand upon him.
And have him stand before Eleazar the priest
and before all the community
and command him before their eyes.
You must put your splendor upon him
so that the people will accept him."
And Moses did to Joshua as Yahweh had spoken.

And now Yahweh said to Moses,
"Say to the Israelites,
'When you cross the Jordan into Canaan,
you shall dispossess the people of the land.
All their carved statues and molten images you shall destroy,
and all their cult places.
And you shall take possession of the land and settle in it,
for I have given you that land to possess.
By the tribes of your fathers you shall take your shares.
But if you do not dispossess the people of the land,
the ones you allow to remain
will become stings in your eyes and thorns in your sides,
and they will assault you in the land where you live.
And it shall come to pass:
As I had thought to do to them, I will do to you."

And then He said,
"Say to the Israelites,'When you enter the land of Canaan,
this is the land you will inherit, by its borders:
on the south, from the wilderness of Zin to the Great Sea;
on the west, the coast of the Great Sea;
on the north, from the Great Sea to Mount Hor to Hazar-enan;
on the east, from Hazar-enan along the Jordan to the Dead Sea.'"

All these teachings Yahweh commanded to the Israelites
by the hand of Moses
in the plains of Moab
by the Jordan River
across from Jericho.

DEUTERONOMY

דברים

MOSES SPOKE TO THE ISRAELITES

In the land across the Jordan, in the wilderness,
Moses spoke to the Israelites.
It was in the fortieth year, on the first day of the eleventh month.

"Yahweh, our God, said to us
when we were in Sinai,
'You have stayed long enough at this mountain.
Go, take the land I promised to your fathers,
to Abraham, to Isaac, and to Jacob,
to them and their children after them.'

And we set out from Sinai and traveled through

the great and terrible wilderness that you saw.

Yahweh heard your complaints against Him and He vowed,

'Not one of these men, this evil generation,

shall see the land that I swore to give your fathers,

none except Caleb, son of Jephunneh.'

Yahweh was angry at me, too, because of you, and He said,

'You shall not enter it, either.

Joshua, son of Nun, who attends you, he will come there,

and you must strengthen him.

And your little ones who do not yet know good from evil,

they shall enter the land. To them I will give it.'"

WE WHO ARE HERE TODAY

And Moses said to the Israelites,

"And now listen to the laws I am teaching you.

Make them known to your children and your children's children.

When you stood before Yahweh at Sinai

and the mountain was blazing with fire and dark with clouds,

Yahweh spoke to you out of the fire.

He said to you the Ten Words,

and He wrote them on two tablets of stone:

Do not make for yourselves sculpted images of a man or woman,

or a bird that flies in the sky

or anything that creeps upon the earth

or a fish in the waters of the sea.

And when you look up at the sky and see the moon and the stars,

do not let yourself be lured away to bow down before them.

For Yahweh took you

and brought you from Egypt, that iron-blast furnace,
to be His people.

"Has there ever been anything like it?
Has any people ever heard the voice of God
coming from the midst of a fire, as you did,
and still lived?
And has any god ever taken one people
from the midst of another
with a mighty hand and an outstretched arm?"

And Moses said,
"Learn the laws I speak and do them always.
Yahweh, our God, made a covenant with us at Sinai.
Not with our fathers did He make it but with us, the living—
we who are here today."

HEAR, O ISRAEL!

"Hear, O Israel!
Yahweh, our God, Yahweh is One.
And you shall love Yahweh, your God,
with all your heart and all your being and all your might.
And these words that I command you today
shall be upon your heart.
You shall teach them to your children,
and speak of them when you are at home and when you are away,
when you lie down and when you rise up.
You shall bind them upon your hand
and wear them as a sign between your eyes.

And you shall write them upon the doorposts of your house
and upon your gates.

"And when Yahweh, your God, brings you to the land
that He swore to your fathers, to Abraham and Isaac and Jacob,
to give to you—
great towns that you did not build,
houses full of good things that you did not fill,
stone cisterns that you did not hew,
vineyards and olive groves that you did not plant—
and you eat and are satisfied,
be watchful.
Do not forget Yahweh.
Trust in Him alone."

A PEOPLE HOLY TO YAHWEH

"And when Yahweh, your God, brings you there,
He will cast out the Hittite and the Girgashite
and the Amorite and the Canaanite
and the Perizzite and the Hivite and the Jebusite—
seven nations more powerful than you.
Yahweh, your God, will give them to you,
and you will strike them down.
Then you must show them no mercy.
Do not allow your daughters and sons to marry theirs,
so that they make your son worship other gods.
Rather you shall smash their altars and shatter their pillars,
cut their sacred trees and burn their idols in fire.

"For you are a people holy to Yahweh, your God.
It is you He chose to be His treasured people.
It is not because you are so many that Yahweh chose you,
for you are the fewest of all people.
No, it was because Yahweh loved you
and kept the oath He swore to your fathers
that He brought you out of Egypt with a mighty hand
and saved you from the house of slaves.

"Remember the long way that Yahweh, your God,
led you these forty years in the wilderness,
to test you by hardship, to learn what was in your hearts—
whether you would keep His commands or not.
He afflicted you with hunger and fed you with manna
to teach you that man does not live by bread alone
but by the Word of God.
So you shall keep the commands of Yahweh,
to walk in His ways and to fear Him.

"Surely this teaching I give you this day
is not too difficult for you, or far away.
It is not in the heavens or beyond the sea.
No, it is very close to you—
in your mouth and in your heart,
to do it.

"Now I set before you life and good,
and death and evil.
And I call heaven and earth as witnesses.
Life and death I set before you:

the blessing and the curse.
Choose life so that you may live.
Love Yahweh, your God;
listen to His voice and cling to Him,
for He is your life and the length of your days."

THE TIME IS COMING

Now Yahweh said to Moses,
"The time is coming for you to die.
Call Joshua and wait at the Tent of Meeting,
so that I might make him ready."
Moses and Joshua came there,
and Yahweh came there in a pillar of cloud.
And He said to Moses,
"Here, you will soon lie beside your fathers,
and this people will abandon Me
and the covenant I made with them,
and turn to other gods.
I know what plans they are devising even now.
But I will give you a song as a witness against them.
Teach it to the Israelites; put it in their mouths."

Then Yahweh commanded Joshua, son of Nun,
"Be strong, be brave,
for you will bring the Israelites to the land I swore to them,
and I will be with you."

And when Moses had finished writing the words of the teaching
in a book to the very end
he charged the Levites who carried the Ark of the Covenant,

"Take this book of teaching and put it
beside the Ark of the Covenant of Yahweh, your God."

LET MY TEACHING FALL LIKE RAIN

And Moses taught Yahweh's song to the Israelites:
        "Heaven and earth, hear me.
        Let my teaching fall like rain,
        like showers on the grass.
        Yahweh's possession is His people.
        Jacob is His inheritance.
        He found him in a wilderness, a howling desert.
        He protected him and cared for him,
        like an eagle guarding its young.
        He set him down in the high country.
        He fed him honey from the crag,
        and oil from the flinty rock.
        Then Israel grew fat and kicked—
        scorning the God who rescued him.

        Yahweh saw and He said,
        'I will hide My face from him,
        sweep evils upon him—
        arrows, plague, and beasts.
        But I fear the taunts of My enemies,
        believing they defeated Israel.
        No, I will relent and
        avenge My fallen people.
        I bring death and give life.
        I wound and I heal,
        and no one can be taken from Me.'"

Moses came, he and Joshua, and sang the words to the end.

That very day, Yahweh spoke to Moses, saying,
"Climb these heights of Abiram to Mount Nebo,
in the land of Moab, facing Jericho,
and see the land of Canaan, which I am giving to the Israelites.
You will die on the mountain and be gathered to your kin,
as Aaron, your brother, died on Mount Hor
because you both betrayed Me
at the waters of Meribah in the wilderness of Zin,
because you did not sanctify Me in the midst of the people.
You will see the land I am giving,
but you will not enter there."

Signs and wonders

Now Moses blessed the Israelites
and he went up from the plains of Moab to Mount Nebo,
to the top of Pisgah that faces Jericho.
And Yahweh let him see all the land,
from Gilead to the Western Sea to the Negev,
and the Valley of Jericho, town of palm trees,
as far as Zoar.
And Yahweh said to him,
"This is the land I swore to Abraham, to Isaac, and to Jacob, saying,
'To your children I will give it.'
I have let you see it with your own eyes,
but you shall not cross over."

And Moses, the servant of Yahweh,
died there in the land of Moab at Yahweh's command.

And he was buried in Moab opposite Beth Peor.
No one knows his burial place to this day.
And Moses was a hundred and twenty years old when he died;
his eyes were clear and his strength had not left him.
The Israelites wept for Moses on the plains of Moab
for thirty days.
And the days of weeping for Moses were ended.

Now Joshua, son of Nun, was filled with wisdom,
for Moses had laid his hands upon him,
and the Israelites followed Joshua
and did as Yahweh had commanded Moses.
But no prophet like Moses again arose
whom Yahweh knew face-to-face,
with all the signs and wonders
Yahweh sent him to do in the land of Egypt.
And Moses did them with a mighty hand
before the eyes of all Israel.

Notes

GENESIS

PAGE 1 ⤳

God called the light Day. And the darkness He called Night.
The pronoun *He* is true to Hebraic translations of the Torah, although for the Israelites, God's divinity was beyond male or female. Today many Jews avoid using pronouns for God in their prayers and synagogue services.

PAGE 3 ⤳

At the time of Yahweh's making of earth and heaven . . .
Yahweh is a phonetic rendering of the Hebrew YHWH, used in place of the more customary *Lord,* with its connotations of property and ownership. In fact, the pronunciation of God's name is forbidden in Judaism, and its meaning is an enduring mystery.

PAGE 6 ⤳

Yahweh was pleased with Abel and his gift.
But He was not pleased with Cain's gift.
In a pattern that will dominate Genesis, the younger brother is chosen over the firstborn: Abel over Cain, Isaac over Ishmael, Jacob over Esau, Joseph over his older brothers, Ephraim over Manasseh. This goes against the ancient practice of primogeniture, in which the oldest son inherits everything.

PAGE 11 ⤳

Noah planted a vineyard and he became drunk from the wine.
He was naked in his tent when Ham entered there and saw him.
This strange story reflects ancient taboos about a parent's nakedness that may involve an act of incest. In the passage that follows this one, Noah, in retribution, curses not Ham but Ham's son Canaan, saying, "A slave shall he be to his brothers." It is a prophecy and perhaps a justification of the Israelites' later conquest of the Canaanites.

PAGE 15 ⤳

And Abram came to dwell near the terebinths of Mamre . . .
Terebinths are small sturdy pistachio trees, prized in a dry region.

PAGE 17 ⌣

Yahweh said,

"Bring Me a young heifer, a she-goat and a ram, a turtledove and a pigeon."

And he brought them.

Abram halved them down the middle and put each part opposite to the other.

Here Yahweh and Abram enter into a covenant sealed by the presence of the halved animals, a legal ritual in the ancient Near East. The term "to cut a deal" may originate from it.

PAGES 17–18 ⌣

"You must know now,

know that your children will be strangers in a land not theirs.

They will be put into slavery and afflicted for four hundred years. . . .

And in the fourth generation, your children will return here."

This passage looks forward to Exodus, prophesying the fate of the Israelites under Pharaoh. Time in the Torah is mutable and often exaggerated. Note the difference between "four hundred years" and "in the fourth generation." It may be that what is called a generation is, instead, the span of a human life.

PAGE 18 ⌣

"Come. Lie with my slave girl so that I may have a son through her."

The practice of using slaves as surrogate mothers to provide infertile women with children is well documented in the ancient Near East.

PAGE 20 ⌣

"Every male among you shall be circumcised at eight days old

so that in your flesh will be

a sign of the covenant between us."

Circumcision was practiced among many Near Eastern peoples but was performed in early adolescence as a puberty rite. By moving circumcision back to the eighth day after birth, the Torah makes the covenant a commitment for life at the same time that it marks every Israelite male.

PAGE 27 ⌣

And now it happened

that God tested Abraham and said to him,

"Abraham!"

And he said, "Here I am."

Abraham's response is frequently used in the Torah to show readiness to act or obey a command; it may also imply a heightened state of consciousness.

PAGE 30

"I am a sojourner and settler among you.

Sell me a burial tomb so that I might bury my dead."

Despite Yahweh's promise of land, Abraham is still landless in Canaan, which is why he wants to acquire a legal and permanent burial plot for Sarah and later himself. Isaac, Rebekah, Jacob, and Leah also are thought to be buried here.

PAGES 30–31

"Put your hand under my thigh, and swear to me by Yahweh,

God of heaven and earth . . ."

Thigh is probably a euphemism for the genitals. In the ancient Near East, holding the genitals or putting a hand next to them was a gesture used when swearing a solemn oath.

PAGE 31

He had the camels kneel down by the water well in the evening,

at the hour when the women came to draw water . . .

The well is a place of meeting, and in the Torah it figures in several betrothals between a stranger and a maiden, including Isaac (through Abraham's servant) and Rebekah, Jacob and Rachel, and Moses and the seven daughters of the priest of Midian. The meeting at the well often involves a feat of strength or compassion from the stranger.

PAGES 48–49

Then Jacob peeled white strips from poplar and almond and plane branches

and set them before the goats.

And the sheep he kept apart, facing all the dark-colored in Laban's flock.

From that time, the goats bore only speckled and spotted goats for Jacob,

and the ewes only dark sheep.

Jacob's maneuver is probably based on the ancient superstition that what a mother sees during pregnancy influences the appearance of her offspring. Thus striped branches seen by goats would produce two-colored kids and dark sheep seen by ewes would produce dark-colored lambs.

PAGE 49

"Our father regards us as strangers

now that he has sold us and used all our bride-price for himself."

This passage implies that the bride-price, a gift from the groom to the bride's father, was usually given to the bride herself. Since Jacob did not pay Laban directly for his daughters, the bride-price referred to is probably Jacob's years of labor.

PAGE 49 ⌐

Their father, Laban, was shearing the sheep,

and Rachel stole his household gods to take with her.

Though Jacob's one God is Yahweh, it seems safe to assume that Rachel and others in Laban's family believed in other gods. Those referred to here were probably small statues kept to protect the household.

PAGE 52 ⌐

"From now on, your name will not be Jacob but Israel: *God wrestler,*

for you have fought with God and men, and won."

God renames Jacob in the same way Abram was renamed earlier. But unlike Abram's new name, *Abraham,* Jacob's new name, *Israel,* is seldom used. *Israel* has been translated in many ways, but "God wrestler" implies a struggle and has been chosen for that reason. From Exodus forward, the descendants of the patriarchs are called Israelites.

PAGE 62 ⌐

And Jacob mourned for his son, ripping his clothes in grief.

This ancient ritual of mourning is still practiced today. When an Orthodox Jewish man learns of the death of a family member, he rips his coat on the left side over the heart. Other Jews wear small ripped black ribbons on their clothing.

PAGE 73 ⌐

And food was passed to them,

but Benjamin's portion was five times more than the others.

Joseph and Benjamin are full brothers, the only children of Jacob's preferred wife, Rachel. Thus Joseph singles out Benjamin for special favors.

EXODUS

PAGE 88 ⌐

Then the woman gave him to Pharaoh's daughter and he became her son

and she called his name Moses, *for she had pulled him from the water.*

Moses, meaning "son of," was a common name in ancient Egypt. In Hebrew, it is a form of the verb "to pull from the water." The name could also refer to Moses's "pulling" the Israelites out of bondage in Egypt.

PAGE 89 ⌒

Moses was herding the flock of his father-in-law, the priest of Midian,

and he led the flock into the wilderness — he came to the mountain of God.

This is Mount Sinai, where Moses later receives God's commandments, though it may already have been known as a sacred place in the region. It is also called Mount Horeb.

PAGE 89 ⌒

Moses hid his face, for he was afraid to look at God.

Adam and Eve see God walking in the garden in Eden, and Abraham, too, encounters God in human form. Jacob sees God in dreams and perhaps in disguise. Moses hears God's voice but sees only fire burning — illuminating and destructive. In the Torah from this time forward, no one will be able to see God.

PAGE 94 ⌒

And Yahweh said to him, "The signs that I have given to you,

you must do before Pharaoh.

But I will harden his heart so that he will not let the people go."

This theme — the "hardening" of Pharaoh's heart, Pharaoh's refusal to give the Israelites their freedom — runs through the plague story in Exodus. The implication is that God is behind it, making Pharaoh willful so that God's power and supremacy over other gods is shown. But it is also true that Pharaoh is a willful tyrant.

PAGE 94 ⌒

At a night encampment on the way,

Yahweh waited for Moses and tried to kill him.

But his wife, Zipporah, circumcised her son

and protected Moses with the blood, saying,

"You are a bridegroom of blood to me!"

This passage is one of the most bewildering in the Torah. Because Moses was brought up as an Egyptian, he probably was uncircumcised, but that does not seem sufficient reason for God to try to kill him. Nor does the fact that Moses has apparently not circumcised his son. Many commentators link this incident with the tenth plague, when the Israelites are told to smear a lamb's blood on their houses so that God will not kill their sons. But it also foreshadows Moses's tragedy at the Waters of Meribah, when he is forbidden from entering Canaan.

PAGE 106

"Seven days shall you eat flatbread,

and when your son asks, 'What does this mean?'

say to him, 'With a mighty hand, Yahweh brought us out of Egypt.'

And you shall keep this festival from year to year

and in every generation."

The festival referred to is Passover, and flatbread is *matzoh.* Fermented beans and grains are forbidden during Passover, which falls in the early spring. At each evening's *seder,* a meal with foods and customs representing aspects of slavery and liberation, the Passover story is retold. The Passover story and the exodus are at the core of Jewish national existence; the command to keep the festival in every generation guarantees the continuance of that nation.

PAGE 114

. . . and as the sun rose and the dew lifted,

there was something white, like frost upon the ground.

The passage then says that this is bread God has given to the Israelites for food in the wilderness. It is called *manna,* and some scholars offer a naturalistic explanation that it's the sweet crystallized secretions of aphids from the sap of tamarisk trees.

PAGE 122

God spoke all these words, saying,

"I am Yahweh, your God,

who brought you out of the land of Egypt,

from the house of slaves."

Following these lines is the first recital of what are commonly called the Ten Commandments. But they are referred to in the Torah as the Ten Words. Perhaps each one could be reduced to a single word, which would explain how they might fit on two stone tablets.

PAGE 122

"Remember the Sabbath day, to keep it holy.

On six days you shall work,

but the seventh day is a Sabbath for Me."

This is the first clear and detailed command to do no work on the Sabbath. Even farm animals and slaves are forbidden to work on the Sabbath. The idea of a day of rest was new in the ancient world, and many might argue that it is a great gift that has come from the Jews.

PAGE 124

"Let the Israelites make Me a Tabernacle
so that I might dwell among them.
There I will speak with you and the Israelites,
and I will sanctify Aaron and his sons to be My priests."

The Tabernacle is a movable sanctuary that allows a nomadic people to bring God with them on their wanderings. It is a place where the Israelites may offer sacrifices, and later the Tabernacle will be carried before them into battle. Aaron and his sons, like Moses from the tribe of Levi, are chosen as God's priests. As such, they are exempted from military campaigns and own no land.

PAGE 126

And Yahweh said, "They are a stiff-necked people,
and My anger will blaze against them."

Repeatedly used in this section of Exodus, *stiff-necked* is a Hebrew term for "headstrong" or "stubborn."

LEVITICUS

PAGE 137

It is a burnt offering, a fire offering to Yahweh.

Detailed in Leviticus are various kinds of offerings or sacrifices to God. These are probably remnants of earlier cultic practices in which animals and grain were offered as actual food for the gods to eat. Animal sacrifice persisted in early Judaism through the destruction of the second temple in Jerusalem in 70 CE.

PAGE 141

"Next, a man who has been chosen shall take the goat
and send it into the wilderness, with the sins of the Israelites upon it.
And the goat shall be set free. . . .
It is a Sabbath of Sabbaths for you, a day of atonement for you.
And you shall be made pure."

The Day of Atonement described in this passage is a once-yearly purification ritual to ensure that God's sanctuary was not defiled. The term *scapegoat* apparently comes from the sending of the goat into the wilderness. The Hebrew name for the Day of Atonement is *Yom Kippur.* It follows New Year's, or *Rosh Hashanah.* Together, the two holidays and the days between them are called the High Holy Days or Days of Awe.

NUMBERS

PAGE 154

> *Then Yahweh's anger rose up,*
>
> *and when the cloud moved away from the Tent,*
>
> *look, Miriam's skin was bleached with snow-white scales.*

This seems to refer to a skin disease that was curable but may have been contagious. Note that in punishment, Miriam is taken from the community, perhaps a form of quarantine.

PAGES 163–164

> *And Yahweh said to Moses and to Aaron,*
>
> *"Because . . . you did not sanctify Me before the Israelites,*
>
> *you shall never lead this community*
>
> *into the land I gave them."*

Scholars have long disputed the reason for the severity of Moses's punishment. But the most likely explanation may be that he has not followed God's orders. Having been told to "speak to the rock so that it will bring forth water," Moses instead strikes it with his staff, so that the miracle seems his rather than God's.

Bibliography

I could never have written this book without the brilliant translations and commentary of three Hebraic editions of the Torah. They are as follows:

Alter, Robert. *The Five Books of Moses.* New York: Norton, 2004.

Berlin, Adele, and Marc Zvi Brettler, editors; Michael Fishbane, consulting editor. *The Jewish Study Bible.* New York: Oxford University Press, 2004. *Jewish Publication Society* TANAKH *Translation.* Philadelphia: The Jewish Publication Society, 1985.

Fox, Everett. *The Five Books of Moses.* New York: Schocken, 1983.

Several books were useful to me in putting the Torah in a broader context:

Armstrong, Karen. *The Bible: A Biography.* New York: Grove Press, 2008.

———. *A History of God.* New York: Ballantine, 1994.

Cahill, Thomas. *The Gifts of the Jews.* New York: Doubleday/Talese, 1998.

Heschel, Abraham Joshua. *God in Search of Man: A Philosophy of Judaism.* New York: Farrar, Straus, 1955.

Johnson, Paul. *A History of the Jews.* New York: Harper Perennial, 1988.

Miles, Jack. *God: A Biography.* New York: Vintage, 1996.

Acknowledgments

I am grateful to the following people, who agreed to read and comment on the manuscript. Their deep knowledge of the Torah and of Judaism were invaluable: Angela Buchdahl, David Buchdahl, Rachel Cowan, and Rob Hirschfeld.

The following people also read the manuscript and gave me important feedback: Emilie Adams, David Conrad, Theresa Del Pozzo, Becky Hemperly, Libby Hillhouse, Henry Ingraham, David Martin, David Noble, and Rachel Siegel.

I am especially indebted to my agent, Joe Spieler, and my editor, Karen Lotz, for their belief in the project and their encouragement while I was working on it. And to Kaylan Adair, Hannah Mahoney, Chris Paul, and Rachel Smith for their help in making the manuscript into a book.

Artist's Note

Religion and art have always been entwined in my imagination. From my earliest memories, they were linked in a way that I did not question. The impulse toward each was the same and the feeling I had while involved in each was of a profound remembering.

So being presented the opportunity to make these paintings for Amy Ehrlich's retelling of the Torah felt like a perfect fit. And it all began with the Word. I was familiar with most of these stories, but some were new to me and very surprising. (Balaam, the sorcerer, springs to mind.) The first six months of the two years it took to complete this project consisted of reading the text over and over and trying to embody these stories with paint and wood.

In every case it was a matter of getting to the essential nature of each scene, without distractions, to let the stories breathe on their own. I dreamt of them often.

The book you hold is my humble offering. I have done my best to live up to the task given me. It continues to feel like a homecoming, a circle completed. I am altered by the journey taken and it is my hope that the reader's imagination is stirred by these remarkable stories.

Daniel Nevins
Asheville, North Carolina